Teaching
with Folk Stories
of the Hmong

LEARNING THROUGH FOLKLORE SERIES
Norma J. Livo, Series Editor

Who's Afraid...? Facing Children's Fears with Folktales. By Norma J. Livo.

Of Bugs and Beasts: Fact, Folklore, and Activities. By Lauren J. Livo, Glenn McGlathery, and Norma J. Livo.

Folktale Themes and Activities for Children, Volume 1: Pourquoi Tales. By Anne Marie Kraus.

Folktale Themes and Activities for Children, Volume 2: Trickster and Transformation Tales. By Anne Marie Kraus.

Teaching with Folk Stories of the Hmong: An Activity Book. By Dia Cha and Norma J. Livo.

Teaching
with
Folk Stories
of the Hmong

An Activity Book

DIA CHA

NORMA J. LIVO

Photographs and art
by Norma J. Livo

2000
Libraries Unlimited, Inc.
Englewood, Colorado

To the Hmong.
May your future always be filled with promise and joy.
—N.J.L.

Libraries Unlimited, Inc.
P.O. Box 6633
Englewood, CO 80155-6633
1-800-237-6124
www.lu.com

Library of Congress Cataloging-in-Publication Data

Cha, Dia, 1962-
     Teaching with folk stories of the Hmong : an activity book / Dia Cha, Norma J. Livo.
        p. cm. -- (Learning through folklore series)
     Includes bibliographical references and index.
     ISBN 1-56308-668-9 (pbk.)
     1. Hmong (Asian people)--Social life and customs--Juvenile literature. 2. Hmong (Asian people)--Folklore--Juvenile literature. 3. Tales--Asia. 4. Hmong (Asian people)--Study and teaching--Activity programs--Juvenile literature. I. Livo, Norma J., 1929- II. Title. III. Series.

DS509.5.H66 C47 2000
305.895'942--dc21
                                                                          00-023227

Contents

FIGURES ix

ACKNOWLEDGMENTS xiii

1—HMONG PEOPLE: ORIGINS AND HISTORY 1

Hmong Origins 1
  Language 1
    Proverbs 2
      Discussion and Activities 2
    Riddles 2
      Discussion and Activities 3
  Physical Appearance 3
Hmong History 4
  Hmong History in Southeast Asia 4
  Hmong History in the West 5
  Hmong History in the United States 5
      Discussion and Activities 6
Dia's Memories 8
  Memories of Escaping 8
  Memories of Village Life 9
  Memories of Refugee Camp Life 13
      Discussion and Activities 14
Issues for Hmong Immigrants Today 14
Notes 16

2—FARMING AND FOOD. 17

Raising Rice 18
        Discussion and Activities 19
Food. 20
   Recipes 24
      Meat Dish 24
      Soup 24
      New Mother's Menu for the First Thirty Days After Giving Birth . . 25
      Discussion and Activities 25

3—STORIES AND STORYTELLING 27

Storytelling. 29
   Telling a Story Successfully 30
The Orphan Boy and His Wife 31
      Discussion and Activities 34
Variations on a Theme 36
High-Tech Cinderella 36
   Bibliography of Cinderella Variants. 38
      Discussion and Activities 39
Two Stories from Two Cultures 39
The Taiga Sampo, or The Magic Mill 40
Zeej Choj Kim, the Lazy Man 45
      Discussion and Activities 49
Love Ghost Story 50
      Discussion and Activities 53

4—WRITING AND ILLUSTRATING STORIES 55

Thoughts on Writing 55
      Discussion and Activities 55
Illustrating Stories. 57
   Paper Cutting 59
   Paper Weaving 59
   Tissue Paper 59
   Tracing Paper 59
   Stenciling. 59
   Rubbings 59
   Finger Printing. 59
   String Block Printing 60
   Polystyrene Printing 60
   Wood Block Printing 60
   Using Other Objects. 60
   Making a Picture Book 60

5—HMONG FOLK ARTS 61
  Pa Ndau 61
    Pa Ndau Samples 62
      Discussion and Activities 62
  String-Tying Ceremony. 62
  Blessing 63
      Discussion and Activities 64
  Jewelry 64
      Discussion and Activities 64
  Creating Textiles. 66
      Discussion and Activities 70
  Traditional Hmong Music and Musical Instruments 70
    Keng 70
    Mouth Harp 73
    Leaf Blowing. 74
    Violin 74
    Flutes 74
    Songs 74
  Contemporary Hmong Music and Musical Instruments 76
      Discussion and Activities 77
  Symbolism in Hmong Folk Art 78
    Symbols of Creatures 78
      Discussion and Activities 80
    Other Symbols. 82
      Discussion and Activities 85
  Colors. 85
      Discussion and Activities 86

6—CUSTOMS AND SYMBOLS 89
  New Year's Festival 89
  Marriage Customs. 90
      Discussion and Activities 91
  Games and Toys. 94
  Kao Xiong's Childhood Memories of Play 94
      Discussion and Activities 97
  Buildings and Homes 98
      Discussion and Activities 98

  BIBLIOGRAPHY 101
    Audio Productions 105
    Video Productions 105
  INDEX 107

Figures

1.1.   *Pa ndau* with the map of Laos. The provinces are marked, and details of the various cultures, clothing, activities, and customs surround the map . . 7

1.2.   Groups of Hmong people wearing clothing specific to each group 7

1.3.   Bamboo water carrier 10

1.4.   An aqueduct carrying water from the mountains. 11

1.5.   Dragons that live in the water 12

2.1.   Daily activities illustrated on a *pa ndau*. 19

2.2.   Dia Cha with her mother and sister 21

2.3.   Herb gardens 21

2.4.   Tall lemongrass plants 22

2.5.   Dia in a herb/vegetable garden. 22

2.6.   Bitter melons 23

3.1.   Fu and Myhnia Ly holding a *pan ndau* with three folktales stitched on it. 28

4.1.   Elements of a story 56

4.2.   Scene from a folktale showing the wife stitching *pa ndau* while her husband is on the rock above as he comes to rescue her from the tigers 57

4.3.   A couple going to gather firewood 58

4.4.   A family on a trail with the baby being carried in the baby carrier on the woman's back. 58

5.1.   *Baci*, or string-tying ceremony. 63

5.2.   Friendship bracelet instructions. 65

5.3.   *Pa ndau* showing cutting the trees; planting hemp seeds; harvesting, drying, and stripping the hemp; winding fiber and spinning it into thread; dying and drying the yarn; weaving fabric; cutting fabric for clothing; sewing clothes, taking crops to the family storage building; and grinding grain into flour 66

5.4.   Stripping the hemp plant to start the fiber-making process 67

5.5.   Winding the fiber 67

5.6.   Spinning the fiber into thread 68

5.7.   Weaving the fabric on the loom 68

5.8.   Cutting pieces from the fabric and sewing them into clothes 69

5.9.   Hmong family takes the garden crops to their storage building 69

5.10.   *Keng* player 71

5.11.   *Keng* player depicted on a *pa ndau* 72

5.12.   Mice playing the funeral *keng* and drum. 72

5.13.   Musician playing the one-string violin. 75

5.14.   One-string violin 75

5.15.   Modern amplified musicians playing for a Hmong New Year's celebration. 76

5.16.   Snail shell, which symbolizes family and growth. 78

5.17.   Centipede, which is valued for its medicinal qualities 79

5.18.   Fireworks and snail shells 79

5.19.   Snail shells and dog foot corners 79

5.20.   Elephant's foot and plume design. The elephant's foot is the imprint of the most powerful good spirit. The plume design is associated with great wealth 81

5.21.   Elephant's foot and dog's foot designs 81

5.22.   Spider web with a variety of borders 81

5.23.   Elephant's foot with diamonds in a square. Diamonds in a square
         can represent an altar or mountains 83

5.24.   Dream maze with the happiness-for-all symbol 83

5.25.   Star with snail shell and heart motif 83

5.26.   Heart design 84

5.27.   Centipede border with crosses and spinning wheel design 84

5.28.   Ram's head, elephant's foot, and heart motif 84

6.1.   Ball playing at the New Year's festival followed by a wedding group . . . 90

6.2.   Wedding ceremonies 91

6.3.   Shaman holding the rooster over the wedding couple to symbolize
         that the bride is now a member of the groom's household 92

6.4.   This healing ceremony with the sacrifice of a pig is another
         important family ritual. The sick person is sitting while the
         shaman performs healing rituals at the family altar 92

6.5.   Two Hmong boys with bows and arrows leaving for the hunt 96

6.6.   Two children chasing chickens 96

6.7.   Boy riding a water buffalo 97

6.8.   Examples of Hmong buildings 99

6.9.   Woman sitting in front of a house 99

Acknowledgments

Friendship Bracelet Instructions, appearing on page 65, are reproduced by permission of The DMC Corporation (107 Trumball Street, Elizabeth, NJ 07206). Copyright © 1987, The DMC Corporation.

Inked graphic representations of *pa ndau* and other Hmong artwork are from *Hmong Textile Designs* by Anthony Chan with an introduction by Norma Livo (Owings Mills, MD: Stemmer House, 1990). Used by permission. This permission is not transferable to any other publisher or publication without further written permission.

1

Hmong People: Origins and History

HMONG ORIGINS

In the early 1920s, Father F. M. Savina, a French Catholic priest and anthropologist, was sent to spread the word of God to the Hmong in Laos and northern Vietnam. After many years of studying Hmong culture, legends, and language, he published his views on the origins of the Hmong people in a book titled *Histoire des Miao*. Savina theorized about Hmong origins by emphasizing three facts: their legends, their language, and their physical appearance. He argued that the Hmong have legends, which are similar to European creation and flood stories, original sin, and the Tower of Babel. This places their origins outside of Asia.

Language

Savina studied and learned the Hmong language. Because the Hmong had no written alphabet, he developed a Romanized Hmong script. Savina classified the Hmong language as a form of the Ural-Altaic family language. The Ural-Altaic is one of the three major Caucasian family languages. Savina believed that a subgroup of the Caucasians who lived in western Russia and central Asia spoke a language similar to that of the Hmong ancestors who also inhabited this region before migrating to Asia.

However, modern linguists disagree with Savina. They assert that the Hmong language is not related to the Ural-Altaic family language or any other major family language. The only language that shares some similar characteristics, they argue, is the Yao language. Even so, most scholars still cannot agree about how to categorize the Hmong language.

Proverbs

Important functions of proverbs are to teach both wisdom and the value of playing with language. Proverbs are an important part of language in every culture. Consider the following Hmong proverbs.

- God sees all. Men see but little.

- We see the pigeon but we don't see his nest. (A pigeon is beautiful, but its nest is a horrible mess.)

- The older brother and his wife are like parents, and parents are like heaven and earth.

- When someone has a debt, he must be kind and speak gently to all from whom he has borrowed. (It's better to do good to them than evil.)

- A man with two wives and ten horses is very rich. (For a farmer, the more workers he has, the more he will be able to produce.)

✔ DISCUSSION AND ACTIVITIES

The proverbs above give a glimpse of what is important in the lives of the Hmong. These values include respecting elders, honesty, and goodness. The Hmong observe and learn from nature.

- As a class, look around and analyze what values are important in your culture. Have students create proverbs from these observations.

- What lessons can we learn from the natural world and its inhabitants?

- Discuss what it is to be "rich." What are the various meanings for this word? Create a proverb relating to "rich."

Riddles

Riddles are part of how we play with language and solve problems. They teach us new ways to look at the ordinary. The following Hmong riddles demonstrate this.

- What looks shiny green at a distance but, up close, is like a pair of chopsticks? (beans)

- What is a bowl that cannot hold water? (a nest)

- What is a short old man with eyes all over his body? (a pineapple)

- From a distance, what looks like a dragon but can please a person? (a house)

- What are five mountains, each having its own roof? (finger nails)

- What is a short, old man with a knife sheath? (a drum)

- What is a small animal that is not a bird but has wings? It is not a rat, but it has ears. (a bat)

- What is a white hen who only knows her way out and doesn't know her way in? (saliva)

- What is a short, old man who carries a cooking pan and walks up and down in a river? (a crab)

✔ DISCUSSION AND ACTIVITIES

- Have students make up several riddles to try with their friends.

- Study riddles and discover which ones your students enjoy the most. Discuss what is it about them that they enjoy.

- Have students interview a variety of people and discover what riddles they know. They can even make a lists of these riddles and compare them with those of their classmates. Are there any riddles common to several lists?

Physical Appearance

The other fact that Savina used to support his theory of Hmong migration is the Hmongs' physical appearance. He argued that the Hmong have a "pale yellow complexion, almost white, their hair is often light or dark brown, sometimes even red or corn-silk blond." A few Hmong even have blue eyes. Savina believed that the Hmong race is a mix between the white and yellow races. Thus, the original Hmong homeland must have been outside of Asia.

To some extent, modern anthropologists agree with Savina. They have noticed that the Hmong have many European traits, especially their facial features, such as narrow faces, aquiline noses, and no epicanthic eyelid fold. The Hmong are classified as "the most Caucasian population in Southeast Asia."

By using Hmong physical features, legends, and language, Savina concluded that the Hmong originated in Mesopotamia, the same location that Western civilization began. Savina believed that the Hmong migrated from Iran to Siberia. They settled in Siberia for a while and then migrated again to northeastern China, where they settled down along the Yellow River valley. Other scholars disagree with Savina because they cannot find Hmong legends similar to those described by Savina.

HMONG HISTORY

It is believed that the Hmong belong to a group of people called the "Man" in early Chinese history. The Man, or Hmong, was the first group to settle along the Yellow River in China. After they had settled, the Han Chinese came along. The Hmong and the Han Chinese were able to live in peace for at least 2,000 years in the valley of the Yellow River. Eventually natural resources became scarce, the population grew, and the fertile land became depleted. It was then that the Hmong and the Han Chinese began to have conflicts. Because the Chinese wrote all of the historical sources, the Hmong were labeled the attackers, rebels, and troublemakers.

At the beginning, the Hmong were winning, but after many brutal battles, they lost. The ancient Chinese authority dispersed all the Hmong into different regions hoping that they would not be able to regroup to challenge the Chinese authority again. In this way, the Hmong would be forced to assimilate into the Chinese culture.

As a result of such a dispersal policy, and after hundreds of years of separation from each other, the Hmong formed distinctive cultural groups with different languages, customs, and environmental adaptations. It is believed that the many tribal groups in China today are the descendants of the Man people.

The Chinese historical annals later reported that the Hmong had spread throughout the mountains of China. When Chinese authorities imposed heavy taxes on them, the Hmong began to rebel against the Chinese government. There were many similar uprisings throughout Hmong history in China.

The Han Chinese believed that the Hmong were barbarians and that their culture was uncivilized; as a result, the Han Chinese felt it was their responsibility to civilize the Hmong by assimilating them into the Chinese culture. The Hmong resisted the efforts of the Han Chinese to suppress them until the last Hmong royal family was executed in Beijing in the 1700s. After this, many Hmong chose to remain in China and abide by Chinese rules while other Hmong fled to Southeast Asia to maintain their independence and their cultural heritage.

Hmong History in Southeast Asia

When the Hmong arrived in Vietnam, Laos, Thailand, and Burma, they settled in the uninhabited highlands. This way, the Hmong felt they could live in peace, but this peaceful period did not last long. When the French came to colonize Southeast Asia, they penetrated Hmong territories. They established government officials to govern and collect taxes from the Hmong. As a result of the heavy taxes levied, in 1918 many Hmong rose up to rebel against the French. This rebellion lasted until 1921, when the French successfully captured the Hmong leader, Pa Chai Vue, and ended the rebellion.

After the French left Southeast Asia in the early 1950s, the Americans, Russians, communist Chinese, and North Vietnamese came along. Both the Americans and the communist Russians recruited the Hmong, Chinese, and Vietnamese to carry out their political activities. The American Central Intelligence Agency (CIA) appointed former general Vang Pao as a leader to recruit Hmong men to fight the communist troops in Laos as a "secret army."

This secret army was fully funded, trained, and supported by the CIA to fight the spread of communism in Laos from 1960 to 1975. The Hmong who supported the CIA were responsible for two things: (1) to rescue American pilots who had been shot down and bring them to safety and (2) to spy and monitor the Ho Chi Minh Trail and report to the CIA headquarters in Laos and South Vietnam on the number of troops and ammunition traveling along the trail on a daily basis. This task was very dangerous. Hmong men were required to live in the jungle for months in order to carry out their tasks.

Hmong people were uprooted from their villages. The majority of men were recruited to be soldiers. Many of them were just twelve or thirteen years old. By the time the war ended in 1975, most of the Hmong families had lost a father or son fighting in the Vietnam War in Laos.

After the CIA pulled out of Laos in 1975, thousands of Hmong who had supported the United States government, fled to Thailand because they were afraid of being persecuted by the new communist regime that took over Laos. When the Hmong arrived in Thailand, they were placed in refugee camps. Many of them resettled in the Western countries. Some of them chose to remain in the Thai refugee camps for more than ten years and then decided to return to Laos. Some sneaked out of the camps to live among Hmong Thai villagers, eventually to become Thai citizens.

Hmong History in the West

In 1975, Hmong refugees from the Thai camps began to resettle in any Western country that would provide them with a home. Consequently, the Hmong are spread all over the world today. About 200,000 Hmong refugees came to the United States. Approximately 10,000 Hmong are living in France. There are an estimated 1,600 Hmong living in Australia and about 1,500 Hmong in French Guyana, 500 in Argentina, and 2,000 in Canada.

Hmong History in the United States

In late 1975, the United States began to admit Hmong refugees. Its original policy was to disperse them across the country so that they would assimilate into American society more quickly than if they were grouped together. At that time, the Hmong did not know anything about American culture, food, beliefs, and values. The reverse was also true: Americans knew nothing about the Hmong.

As Hmong refugee families arrived in the United States, they experienced many difficulties and cultural shocks. A Hmong family in the Midwest committed suicide due to isolation and the challenges of adjusting to their new life. Hmong families also moved to join their families or clan in other states. This incident made the United States government reconsider its dispersal policy. After that, Hmong were allowed to resettle where they had relatives.

The larger Hmong communities in the United States today are in California (70,000), Minnesota (40,000), and Wisconsin (30,000). Smaller Hmong communities, which have a few hundred to a few thousand people, are in Arkansas, Colorado,

Texas, Oklahoma, Iowa, Nebraska, Montana, Washington state, Oregon, North and South Carolina, Georgia, Florida, Washington, D.C., Connecticut, Rhode Island, New York, Michigan, Indiana, Illinois, Massachusetts, Pennsylvania, and Ohio.

✔ DISCUSSION AND ACTIVITIES

- ◆ Place pins in a map of the United States to mark the states where the Hmong have settled.

- ◆ Have students ask their relatives about the Vietnam War. Did any of them fight in it? If so, where, when, and in what branch of the armed forces?

- ◆ Students could also interview some Vietnam veterans and collect stories of their lives in the war. Have them ask if the veterans knew about the Hmong during the war. Compile their stories, along with pictures, if possible, in a classroom or library collection for others to see.

- ◆ Introduce students to other books about the Hmong.

- ◆ On a world map, trace the migrations of the Hmong from ancient times.

- ◆ Have students ask their parents about their country or countries of origin. Some questions to include: When did your ancestors come to the United States? Where did they settle? Are there any family stories about their immigration? What kinds of work did they obtain when they settled here?

- ◆ Using a map of the world, have your students mark the countries their families came from.

- ◆ Ask your students if their families spoke another language before moving to the United States.

- ◆ Have students invent their own language and teach it to someone else. Discuss how difficult this was to do and have them describe the steps they used.

- ◆ As a class, create a mural based on the Hmong folk stories.

- ◆ Set up a center in your classroom about the Hmong culture. Include books, maps, drawings, story cloths (*pa ndau*, pronounced *pan-dow'*, sometimes spelled *paj ntaub*), and other items. (See figures 1.1 and 1.2.) Invite speakers.

- ◆ Discuss history, art, and customs of the Hmong.

- ◆ To find Hmong resource people who might be interested in speaking to your class, call your public library.

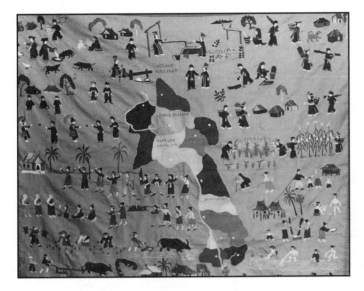

Fig. 1.1. *Pa ndau* with the map of Laos. The provinces are marked, and details of the various cultures, clothing, activities, and customs surround the map.

Fig. 1.2. Groups of Hmong people wearing clothing specific to each group.

DIA'S MEMORIES

> Memory is what gives humanity its face, its pace.
> It gives humanity its reason for hope.
> —Elie Wiesel

Memories of Escaping

Back in Laos, when I was still a child, many things happened that I never understood. I thought the whole world was at war. Of course we had no TV or map, so whatever image of the world I had was mostly my imagination.

Ever since I could remember, my family, relatives, and a lot of other Hmong people were always escaping the communist soldiers. We moved from one village to another and from one province to the next. We were not able to live in a home or a village for more than three years. Every time we settled down, the communist soldiers came and we had to move again. We would leave everything we owned behind, including the animals, our houses, and our fields of rice, corn, and vegetables.

Many times we had to get up in the middle of the night to escape. It was so dark that I could not see anything, but I could hear gun shots everywhere. My mother kept telling my brothers, sisters, and me to hurry up. We were shaking because of fear. We just went wherever other people went. Sometimes we escaped to another village. Many times we went to hide in the forest or nearby mountain caves.

The forest was scary because it had all kinds of creatures living there. There were snakes, birds, insects, bears, wild pigs, deer, and tigers. At night, some of these animals made scary noises.

My father was a soldier, so he was rarely home with my family. One time, the communist soldiers invaded our village right after dark. My father had come to visit us that evening, and he had to flee quickly into the jungle so the communist soldiers could not capture him. All of the men in the village who were soldiers for the non-communist side also fled.

My mother grabbed two blankets and rushed us into the jungle. I remember that it seemed we were walking the whole night, but we found ourselves right on the edge of the village the next morning. There were communist soldiers everywhere. We had to surrender ourselves. If we had run, they might have shot us.

A lot of women and children, like us, were lost on the communist side for a whole year. I remember this particular year as the longest year in my life. It was also one of the most difficult years for my mother. Every time she saw an airplane fly high up in the sky, tears would pour down her face. She just did not know what the future would hold.

We had a rice field located in the middle of the jungle. My mother and a couple of other relatives built houses in the middle of this field and moved us there to live. My mother just told the communist soldiers that we went to farm in our field. She and my relatives brought their animals and their belongings to our house in the field a little at a time. As time passed, we returned to the village less frequently.

One day, one of my sisters and I returned to the village with my mother. My sister and I were playing outside the house when two communist soldiers walked straight toward us and started to ask about our father. One of them asked me, "Where is your father?" I was so afraid that I did not say a word. I just stared at them with my eyes open really wide while my sister ran to our mother.

One of the soldiers continued, "Was your father a soldier? Have you seen him recently?" My face must have turned red because I was feeling quite hot. I did not know how I was going to get away from them, so I just started to cry out really loudly. Then the two soldiers started to walk away from me. After this, I always stayed close to my mother. I was very afraid that the soldiers would grab me and take me away.

I remember seeing my mother taking some of our precious things—silver bars, silver coins, jewelry, and new clothes—to hide in a cave in the forest. When we needed to use some of these things, she would bring one or two of us children with her to the cave and get what she needed. After we finished using the item, we would return it to the cave.

After we had lived in our farmhouse for a few months, rarely returning to the village, the communist soldiers often came to visit us in the field. We had an uncle who was mentally disabled, and we did not think the communist soldiers would bother him. To our surprise, one day they came and tied him with his hands twisted on his back and wanted to take him away. He was the only man with us. My grandmother, my mother, and my uncle's wife all cried and begged them to set him free. They offered the soldiers our pigs, chickens, and dogs in return.

My grandmother told the soldiers that my uncle was mentally ill and that he would not be of any use to them. She and my aunt begged and begged with tears pouring down their faces. Finally, the soldiers set my uncle free. They took one of our pigs, a few of our chickens, and one of our dogs to kill for food.

A few days later, another group of communist soldiers came to check on us. One of my sisters and I had gone to fetch water. When we returned, the soldiers were standing around our front door. I saw my mother feeding chickens nearby. My grandmother and my aunt were talking to the soldiers, and there was yet another woman carrying a backpack basket and walking slowly up the hill. I knew we only had three women—my mother, grandmother, and my aunt. I could not figure out who this woman walking up the hill was. I went to my mother and asked, "Who is that lady?"

She replied quietly, "Just keep your mouth shut."

I was still very curious, so I walked up the hill to have a closer look at this lady. When I got closer, I realized it was my uncle. My mother and my aunt had dressed him up like a woman so he would not be in trouble. I thought to myself, *These people are very clever. I wish to be that clever, like them, when I grow up.*

After talking to my grandmother for a while, the soldiers left. My uncle was free of trouble.

Memories of Village Life

I lived in many villages in Laos. There were too many to count or remember. Most of these villages had no electricity, no paved roads, no indoor toilets, and no noises of machinery.

When I was six or seven years old, I raised a mother chicken that had several baby chicks. I also had a pig that my mother gave to me when it was still a baby. I raised it for a few months, and it grew big and fat. The pig was so cute.

Everyday I would prepare food for my animals. For the chickens, I just threw dry corn and rice for them to eat, but for the pig, I had to go to the forest with my mother to gather and carry home the tender banana leaves and other plants that pigs just love to eat. I would chop the leaves, boil them, add a little rice and corn, and then feed my pig. Oh, it looked delicious, and my pig just ate and ate without raising its head until all the food was gone. I fed my animals twice a day like this. When my chickens grew big, my mother would kill one of them for food. I got to eat a big drumstick as a reward because it was my chicken.

Some days, I would go to the field with my mother and brothers and sisters. On other days I got to stay home with my grandmother. She was very old, and it was hard for her to see things. She would sit by the fire pit or by the front door and tell me to do this and that. One of the things that I usually had to do when I stayed home with her was to dry the rice in the sun. After breakfast, my grandmother would tell me to get the big mat made from woven bamboo. I would spread the mat out in the front yard, carry rice in my little backpack basket (*kawm*) from the rice storage bin inside the house, and spread the rice evenly on the bamboo mat to dry.

After I put the rice in the sun, my grandmother would let me rest and play for a little while. Then she would ask me to bring our bamboo water carrier (*raj dej*) that sat in a corner of the house. I would just carry a small one that was not too heavy for me so that I could fetch the water (see figure 1.3).

Fig. 1.3. Bamboo water carrier.

Sometimes the bamboo aqueduct (figure 1.4) that brought the water down from the hills was broken, so I would have to fetch water from the river. Once, I went to the river for water and saw a fish under a rock. I tried to catch it, but it swam under another rock. As I moved the second rock, it went under a third rock. The fish seemed to be playing hide and seek with me. I was having so much fun that I forgot to return home for a long time.

Fig. 1.4. An aqueduct carrying water from the mountains. This picture also shows someone filling a bamboo water carrier and another fellow on the trail carrying water in the bamboo carrier.

My grandmother was worried about me. When I got home I knew she was not happy. I explained to her that I was just trying to catch a fish but that it kept swimming away from me. She did not say much except to tell me to hurry and finish my task.

Then she said, "Let me tell you a story." I was thrilled. My grandmother told me a story about a dragon that lived in the river (see figure 1.5). She said the dragon was a huge snake. It knew how to transform into all kinds of creatures including human beings and animals like fishes, crabs, and birds. The dragon had magical powers. It could make the water rise higher and higher when it wanted to. When the dragon was angry, it would shake its tail, and the sky would turn dark and begin to thunder and rain. If it continued to shake its tail, then the mountains and land would begin to slide.

My grandmother explained that in Laos there are so many rainstorms, thunderstorms, and landslides during the monsoon season because it is the time of year when the dragons are most unhappy about their lives. They are not able to stay still. They twist, turn, shake their tails, and roll all over the river.

She said the fish that I was trying to catch could be the dragon, who just transformed into a fish to attract me. If I kept chasing it deeper and deeper into the water, the dragon could pull me in. Because there was no one around, even if I yelled, no one would hear me or come to rescue me. If I drowned, then my soul and spirit would go live with the dragon. Then every year during July and August—the monsoon season in Laos—I too would be unhappy like the dragons.

This story scared me enough that I never again attempted to catch a fish in the river alone.

Fig. 1.5. Dragons that live in the water.

Memories of Refugee Camp Life

In 1975, my family escaped to Thailand. When my family got off of the boat that carried us across the Mekong River between Laos and Thailand, I saw my mother look back toward Laos with tears streaming down her face. She said, "My dear mother, I may never see her again." We had left my grandmother behind in our house in the village. She was too old to escape. My mother's older sister was going to take my grandmother to live with her. Because my grandmother had always lived with us, she was extremely sad when we left her. She encouraged us to escape, as my two older brothers and an older sister had already fled to Thailand.

Two weeks after we arrived in Thailand, some of our relatives came and told us that my grandmother had committed suicide. She died alone in our house. A few days before she died, she was talking to one of my aunts and told her that she missed us so much that she did not want to live any longer in this troubled world. When we heard about her death, we all cried. That was the only thing we could do.

As we walked farther from the Mekong riverbank, two Thai soldiers greeted us warmly. "Welcome to Thailand," they said. They took us to an office and wrote down our names. When that was done, we were sent to a refugee camp. I was eleven or twelve years old at the time. (I don't know exactly how hold I was then because I have never known my birthday. In Hmong culture we do not celebrate birthdays every year.) Before we came to the United States, we lived in three different refugee camps in Thailand.

The first was Nong Khai refugee camp. This camp was just across the Mekong River from Laos. When we arrived, there was no shelter for us to live in. My mother bought three bamboo trees from a nearby Thai village and two big plastic sheets from the market. She used the bamboo to make three arcs on the ground. Then she placed one plastic sheet over the arcs and tied both sides down on the ground. She spread another plastic sheet on the ground inside the arcs for us to sleep on. This was our first new home. It was an arc tent that looked like a covered wagon.

When it rained, we just huddled inside our little tent. Sometimes when it rained hard, I could feel the water under the plastic sheet that we sat and slept on. We cooked, cleaned, and carried out most of our daily activities outside of the tent. We had no school in this camp. Our rice was distributed to us once every two weeks. We also received about a pound of meat and a pound of vegetables per person each week. We lived in Nong Khai refugee camp for a few months, and then we were sent to another camp. We were joined there by my older brothers and sister.

The second camp that we lived in was called Ban Na Phong. It was a military training base for Thai soldiers, and my father had trained there once. This camp had barbed wire fence around it, and we were not allowed to leave.

There were wild dogs that lived in the surrounding woods, and they would come out at night. Their eyes gleamed green in the dark. Their barks were scary. Worse than that, these dogs had rabies. If anyone was bitten by them, he or she would die.

It was boring living in the refugee camps. Hmong women busied themselves with traditional needlework or *pa ndau*. Most men had nothing to do except just sit around talking to each other or helping with the baby-sitting. There was a small building designated as a primary school in Ban Na Phong camp. Not all of the children got to attend school because it was crowded. We lived in this camp for almost two years.

Later, we were transferred to Ban Vinai camp, where we lived until we came to the United States. This camp was bigger and had more open space. It was a new camp that had been built to shelter us. We were allowed to leave the camp to make small gardens or find farming work with the Thai villagers. When we left the camp, we were taking a risk. A few men were killed, and several women were raped. When we went outside of Ban Vinai camp, we always traveled in large groups. We lived at Ban Vinai until we came to the United States in 1979.[1]

✔ DISCUSSION AND ACTIVITIES

♦ Have students tell or write a story titled "My Wonderful Day," imagining that they are children in Laos. What makes the day wonderful? How is it like a wonderful day in your students' real lives? How is it different?

♦ Many of the Hmong *pa ndau* illustrate the escape of the Hmong from Laos to Thailand after the United States pulled out of the Vietnam War. Many of the people who escaped were forced to live on what they could find to eat in the jungle. Ask your students: If you were forced to survive on what you found available near your home, what would you eat? How would you cook or prepare it?

ISSUES FOR HMONG IMMIGRANTS TODAY

Today there are many issues concerning the Hmong communities in the United States, and different generations of Hmong experience different challenges and struggles. For the great-great grandparents who fled from China, their struggles were to maintain the cultural traditions and identity that their ancestors had fought so hard to preserve for thousands of years and to deal with the invading foreigners—French, Chinese, Vietnamese—who attempted to trade, colonize, and proselytize them. The parents of today's Hmong youth spent their own youth and their adult lives involved with war, escaping, and becoming refugees in foreign lands.

The challenges and opportunities that the new generation of Hmong faces are quite different from those of their ancestors. Their ancestors came to the United States without much education or experience living an urban life and without financial support for building a new life, yet they came with open minds and open hearts. Amazingly, they have always attempted to regard their present lives as better than the past, otherwise the road of losses and changes would make it impossible to proceed.

Considering the short time the Hmong have been in the United States, and that at least 80 percent of their parents were illiterate when they first arrived, progress has been hard won. When the Hmong first arrived in this country, only one Hmong had received his Ph.D. Now there are about eighty Hmong who have doctorate and advanced professional degrees and work for many mainstream organizations. There are at least 200 Hmong who have received a master's degree in a variety of fields. Hmong women earned about 10 to 15 percent of these advanced degrees. More than 2,000 Hmong have completed bachelor's degrees, and approximately one-third of them are women. Hmong women are taking on many nontraditional roles and are becoming doctors, lawyers, directors, authors, professors, and other types of professionals. Never before in their history have they had this kind of opportunity or achievement.

Other cultural changes include the elimination of the practices of forced, arranged marriages. Young people are free to choose who they will marry. Hmong couples are learning to express their feelings to each other more than they did in the past. While the trend to marry at any early age still exists, many Hmong youths postpone getting married until they finish college or have full-time employment.

Many Hmong parents are now encouraging and treating their daughters in the same ways as their sons. Hmong male professionals are respecting the abilities and achievements of their female counterparts. Young families are learning to juggle and balance child care with jobs in a cooperative way.

There is a trend for Hmong to become more acculturated and to learn to think of their individual desires more than those of their families or clans. With this has come problems. In Laos, Hmong teenagers marry at thirteen or fourteen years of age. There, Hmong youths go from childhood directly into adulthood. There is no teenage status, thus they are either children or adults. Just as their American counterparts, Hmong teenagers in the United States now know more American heroes than Hmong heroes. They are caught between two cultures and the expectations of each.

The Hmong are struggling, accepting challenges, and succeeding in life in the United States. The Hmong culture is adapting and changing with this acculturation. Consider some of the following issues facing the Hmong in their new world today:

- Hmong families are falling apart due to infidelity and individual interests and desires that override the family's well-being. There is a lack of respect for the elderly, parents, and authority figures.

- In the 1980s, only the Hmong girls married very young. Today though, Hmong males are also marrying early.

- Traditionally, only Hmong males could divorce their wives, but today, in America, a Hmong woman can also divorce her husband.

- Traditionally, Hmong men never committed suicide, but in America both Hmong men and women commit suicide.

- Hmong youth listen more to their friends and peers than to their parents and family members.

- Hmong women are taking nontraditional roles by working outside of the home.

- Some Hmong speak no English whereas others have earned college degrees.

- There are some Hmong who still believe and maintain their animist religion while others have converted to Christianity.

- Some Hmong prefer shamans rather than medical doctors.

- The Hmong do not want to be treated as second-class citizens or be stereotyped.

NOTES

1. For more stories of Dia, read her book *Dia's Story Cloth: The Hmong People's Journey of Freedom*, stitched by Chue and Nhia Thao Cha, New York: Lee and Low, 1996.

2
Farming and Food

An important part of Hmong memories from life in Southeast Asia involves farming. Rice has been the major Hmong crop for many generations, where a slash-and-burn style of clearing the fields is used. When the soil's nutritive value is depleted, the Hmong move to new areas.

The following story, "Raising Rice," was written almost twenty years ago by some third-grade Hmong youngsters who were new to the United States. They did not know about books, yet here they were in a Denver public school classroom, and the teacher, Paula Nelson, was to teach them to read. The Hmong had no written language until the 1950s. Without any previous experiences with books, how would the teacher teach them to read? Easy.

When she brought her dilemma to a graduate class at the University of Colorado at Denver, Paula was advised to tap into the Hmongs' life experiences. The assignment was to ask the children to tell her a story about life in Laos, write it down, and have the students draw illustrations for this story. The next step was for the students to make a book of their story, photocopy it for each person in the class, and use this material for their reading lessons. The children saw that what they said could be written down, illustrated, and bound into a book that could be read by others. Talking, reading, and writing were real.

The lesson was such a success that Paula gathered more stories and made a classroom collection of them. This collection included memories, folk stories, and creative writing. Here is the story of "Raising Rice."

Raising Rice

Before we plant the rice we must clear the fields. We use an ax or knife to cut the trees. We use a shovel to clear the land and make it smooth. We let the trees dry in the sun for several months. Then we burn the trees that we have cut.

After we plant the rice seeds, we check on the rice every day.

There is an insect called the *kooj*, or grasshopper, that eats the rice. We have to catch the grasshopper. We catch the grasshoppers at night with a light and put them in a bamboo basket with a top. We also spray the fields.

When the rice is tall, the birds eat it, so the men use a *hneev*, crossbow, to kill the birds that eat the rice.

When the top of the rice plant curves down, the rice is ready to cut. We cut the tops off of the plants. The men and women shake a flat bamboo basket. The leaves fall on the ground and the rice stays on the flat basket.

The rice is stored in a big bamboo storage bin. When the family needs rice to cook for food, they get rice from the bamboo bin.

The women put the rice seeds in a big round wooden barrel. The barrel has a long pole on one side. The women step on one end and make it move like a hammer. The hammer hits the rice seed and knocks the rice off of the shell, and then it is ready to cook.

Fig. 2.1. Daily activities illustrated on a *pa ndau*.

✔ DISCUSSION AND ACTIVITIES

- Discuss with your students what they think the authors of this story might be doing now that it is more than twenty years later.

- Ask students: If your family grew corn, how would you protect it from ravaging birds and other "pests"?

- Have students interview local farmers and find out how they protect their crops from harmful bugs. Share these stories. These stories from the farmers could also be illustrated and bound into a book, *Farmers Fight Against Crop Destruction*.

- In *Folk Stories of the Hmong*, read the story "Why Farmers Have to Work So Hard" (pages 47–53). This story explains why farmers must leave their homes, walk to their fields, harvest their crops, and carry them back home. Then have students write a story about how/why something is as it is today.

◆ Create a class book that is a collection of these farmer stories. After the stories have been written, how can they be organized for this group project? How can you share them with others?

◆ Read the "Legend of the Rice Seed" from *Folk Stories of the Hmong* (pages 34–35). Ask and discuss with your students: Why do you think this story is an important one for Hmong farmers in Southeast Asia?

◆ Have students write or tell their own stories about a grain that grows in your state. Explain who grows it and where as well as how it is grown. What is special about it?

FOOD

Traditionally, Hmong food consists of rice, corn, meat, vegetables, herbs and spices, fruits, bamboo shoots, wild mushrooms, and fish. Rice and vegetables are eaten everyday in Laos as well as in the United States. Pork, beef, and poultry are eaten when they are available in Laos, but most Hmong eat these meats daily in the United States.

In Laos, corn is steamed when it first ripens and is then eaten as a snack. After corn has been dried, harvested, and stored away, it is used to feed the animals, such as pigs, chickens, and ducks. The Hmong usually process dry corn to eat if there is no rice available.

The Hmong in Laos live in the highlands where fish are scarce. However, in places where fish are available, such as near rivers and streams, fish are frequently eaten.

The Hmong eat all kinds of green vegetables, including cabbage, lettuce, bok choy, green mustard, the tender tips of pumpkin vines, and black nightshade. These vegetables are cooked in a variety of ways. The cabbage, bok choy, and green mustard can be steamed, boiled, stir-fried, and pickled. The pumpkin vine tips can only be steamed, boiled, and stir-fried. It cannot be pickled. The tender stems and leaves of black nightshade are boiled into a soup most of the time. People eat the boiled black nightshade with its broth. No salt or sugar is added. This is a dish that older people like. (It is often joked that one knows when a person is old if he or she likes to eat black nightshade soup.)

In addition, the Hmong eat a lot of green beans, turnips, squashes, pumpkins, cucumbers, bamboo shoots, and wild mushrooms. Again, these foods can be steamed, stir-fried, or boiled. All of the above foods can be cooked either as a plain dish (*tsuag*) or a dish with salt, oil, and meat (*qab*).

The Hmong also cultivate many kinds of herbs. Some of these have medicinal properties and must be cooked in a specific way and eaten during a specific occasion, whereas others can be incorporated into daily diets and cooking styles. For example, during the first thirty days after a woman gives birth to a new baby, she can eat only warm rice with chicken soup that has been boiled with special herbs that will help her recover. One of these herbs, lemongrass, is also used in regular, everyday meals. (See figures 2.3–2.6).

Fig. 2.2. Dia Cha with her mother and sister.

Fig. 2.3. Herb gardens.

Fig. 2.4. Tall lemongrass plants.

Fig. 2.5. Dia in a herb/vegetable garden.

Fig. 2.6. Bitter melons.

The Hmong cultivate and eat many kinds of culinary herbs and plants. Cilantro, mint, and other others are traditionally prepared with hot peppers and green onions as a side dish. People sometimes mix this with rice, soup, stew, or stir-fried foods according to their preferences and tolerance of hot peppers. However, since the 1960s, when the Hmong were uprooted from their traditional villages, they have borrowed from many other neighboring tribes' diets. These spices, herbs, and plants then are used in soups, salads, and stir-fried dishes.

The Hmong consider some foods to be symbolic, thus they are more appropriate to serve on certain occasions but not on others. For example, during a wedding, no vegetable is served because the vegetable symbolizes being poor. No hot pepper is served either because the Hmong believe that it will make the marriage hard to manage or that the couple will tend to have heated arguments over little things—just like the hot pepper—once you eat a little, it burns all over your mouth.

During a funeral, the family of the deceased is responsible for providing food for all of the mourners. It is a very sad time, so the food is prepared in a simple manner. The animals that have been sacrificed for the deceased are cooked in soups to feed the guests. No vegetable or any elaborate or gourmet dish is prepared.

The special foods prepared for the New Year's holiday are purple sticky rice, tofu, and meat (beef, pork, and poultry). Because it takes a lot of time to make tofu, the Hmong prepare it mostly during the New Year's celebration. Meat symbolizes wealth and prosperity in Hmong society; therefore an ample amount of meat is consumed during the New Year's holiday.

There are also specific diets prescribed for people who are sick. For instance, it is believed that someone who is sick should not eat garlic, onion, cucumber, hot pepper, and any vegetables or fruits that are sour. Sick people should eat only boiled and steamed food, no stir-fried, malodorous, or oily food.

Recipes

One pleasant summer afternoon I observed the herb and spice collection from the garden and watched the preparation of three traditional Hmong meals by my co-writer, Dia, and her husband, Kao Xiong. Then came the tasty part, when we sampled these foods.

Dia and Kao cooked like my mother-in-law did—a handful of this, a pinch of that, a dash of this, and approximated amounts of water. However, I have recorded these recipes using measuring instructions that are much more formal. A variety of meats and other ingredients can be substituted in each of the recipes .

❦ Meat Dish

2 pounds ground lamb or pork, beef, chicken, or fish

Oil to prevent pan from sticking

2 handfuls chopped fresh cilantro
(approximately ¾ cup)

1 teaspoon salt

¼ cup chopped fresh green onions

Black pepper to taste

4 teaspoons sticky rice powder (slowly roast the sticky rice until it is a golden brown, then grind it into a powder)

1 teaspoon fresh chopped chili pepper, optional

2 tablespoons of fish sauce (available at Asian markets and in some grocery stores)

Juice of ½ lime or lemon

In a large skillet, fry the meat in the oil and stir until cooked. Remove from the heat and add the cilantro, salt, onions, black pepper, sticky rice powder, chili pepper, and fish sauce. Squeeze the lime juice over the mixture. Mix this all together and serve.

❦ Soup

1 quart water

2 handfuls of Hmong vegetables, chopped (cabbage, green beans, squash, pumpkin, broccoli, or cauliflower—whatever is in season)

Combine all the ingredients in a medium-size pot. Cover. Simmer until cooked. Serve hot.

❦ New Mother's Menu for the First Thirty Days After Giving Birth

2 quarts water
1 stalk lemongrass
1 chicken, or a turkey or a Cornish hen
Cilantro
Green onions
Salt and black pepper to taste

Add all the ingredients to a large pot. Cover. Bring to a boil. Reduce the heat and simmer until cooked. Skim off the chicken scum. Remove the chicken and cut it into small pieces. Serve the chicken with steamed rice. The broth can be drunk either hot in winter or cool in the summer.

✔ DISCUSSION AND ACTIVITIES

- Begin a discussion about special foods that your students eat at family reunions. Is there a special dish certain people bring to these events? For instance, does Aunt Virginia always bring her special cole slaw?

- Brainstorm what foods are associated with various holidays. For example, do your students relate watermelons with the Fourth of July? What about birthdays, Thanksgiving, religious holidays, New Year's, or funerals? Compare lists of foods. How are they alike or different?

- Have students keep a list of the foods they eat for a week. They should explain how the food was prepared (baked, fried, boiled, etc.). Were home-cooked meals different from meals eaten away from home? If so, how? Why? Students can compare weekly diets with their classmates and identify and discuss the similarities and differences.

- What are your students' favorite foods? Why? Where and by whom is it fixed?

- Invite a dietitian to visit your class to discuss balanced diets. Did you learn anything you didn't know before?

- Are there regional foods particular to where you live? (These might include such items as scrapple, grits, biscuits and gravy, and vegetables.)

- Visit a garden center and find out what vegetables grow well in your area. If possible, plant your own garden and grow some exotic plants as well as common ones. Share the results with family and friends.

- Ask students if there are any dishes their families cook for good luck, such as corned beef and cabbage on St. Patrick's Day and sauerkraut on New Year's Day.

- Find out what crops are grown by farmers in your area. What are their uses?

- Ask your students: When you are ill, is their a particular dish you are given, such as the popular remedy of chicken soup and rice? What about liquids you are given when sick? Do you eat or drink these items on a regular basis?

- Conduct some research at a health-food store to discover what herbs and other remedies they sell. If possible, after this research, invite a panel of health-care professionals, such as a nurse or doctor, a dietitian, and an herbalist, to discuss the benefits and drawbacks of these products with the class.

- Have students research any plants that are native to your area that are considered medicinal.

- Have students research what plants the Native Americans used for healing.

3

Stories and Storytelling

Stories and music were the first attempts to order chaos. How else can you explain the similarities between the folk stories of people throughout the world? Each story reflects what people were examining, what puzzled them, what was important in their world, and how they explained things.

The stories from *Folk Stories of the Hmong* are like folk stories from any culture. Stories of events and peoples that are remembered—historical or embellished—are part of all of us. There is none among us who is too old or too sophisticated to be touched by a story. As proof of this, consider the case of Kassie S. Neou of the Cambodian Survivors Association who was held prisoner by the Khymer Rouge, the Cambodian Communist party. At an address at the Denver Museum of Natural History, he remembered: "I was taken to jail in 1976 because I spoke three words of English. That was my crime. I survived execution just because guards wanted to keep me alive to tell them stories—Aesop stories."

Some say that stories make us more human. They help us live more lives than we have. Stories help us see the world from inside the skins of people different from ourselves. They help develop compassion and insight into the behavior of ourselves and others. A good story can show us the past in a way that helps us understand the present. One of the most important features of a story is that it develops the imagination. Stories also help us entertain ideas we never could have had without them. Stories are magical: They can take us out of ourselves and return us to ourselves a changed—self-transforming power (figure 3.1).

Fig. 3.1. Fu and Myhnia Ly holding a *pa ndau* with three folktales stitched on it.

Stories can be used to build self-confidence and persistence, to impart values and hopes, to demonstrate follies and triumphs, and to develop an optimistic outlook on life and show the listener or the reader that he or she is not the only one who has ever experienced problems. There is no such thing as a story being only a story.

Ancient stories are the best stories because they have been worked on over the ages by the "folk." Folk stories, or fairy tales, are simply essential to the development of children. The seemingly simple folk story is a combination of entertainment, history, astronomy, religion, literature, and social and natural science. The eminent child psychologist Bruno Bettelheim felt that folk stories teach children that they have to meet danger or do battle, and that only in this way will they grow up.

There have always been people who would avoid these stories or sanitize them. According to Bettelheim, Charles Dickens expressed scorn for those wishing to ban folktales because "Dickens understood that the imagery of fairy tales helps children better than anything else in their most difficult and yet most important and satisfying task: achieving a more mature consciousness to civilize the chaotic pressures of their unconscious." Bettelheim goes on to say:

> Each fairy tale is a magic mirror which reflects some aspects of our inner world, and of the steps required by our evolution from immaturity to maturity. For those who immerse themselves in what the fairy tale has to communicate it becomes a deep, quiet pool which at first seems to reflect only our own image; but behind it we soon discover the inner turmoil of our soul—its depth, and ways to gain peace within ourselves and with the world, which is the reward of our struggles.

Because they are closer to the original oral telling, Hmong stories retain the unsanitized richness of the culture. They have not been edited and censored because of possible offensive elements. They are real!

The ability to tell stories—by the ancient peoples as well as today's suburbanites— is the only art that exists in all human cultures. It is through stories that we experience our lives. The ability to story is what sets people apart from all the other creatures of the earth. It may be the one element that defines us as humans.

A great story is something that one cannot step into twice at the same place, somewhat like Heraclitus's river from mythology. That is the reason for the use of stories in relation to helping children grow and develop. Children find in stories something to build on for future experiences—different spots in the river. Stories are how we contemplate reality and the lessons in life and death.

People have used stories to explain how things should be, the way to behave properly, how things came to be, as well as how the world was created. The layers of meanings in a story fit the level of understanding of each particular listener and reader. We can go back to the same story and discover much more in it at different stages of our lives. The basic function of stories is to help children and adults remain true to themselves on the long journey that is the human experience.

STORYTELLING

In Laos, the Hmong told stories at night, usually beside the fireplace before bedtime. Oral literacy was around a long time before stories were printed in books. Originally the Hmong told their stories in rhymed verse. This storytelling was for anyone who wished to listen.

The Hmong believe that it is not good to reveal all that there is to know about something, therefore no one makes a point of explaining the stories' meanings. Listeners soon realize that Hmong stories tell more than what is apparent on the surface. Their deeper meanings and allusions to religious and philosophical thoughts are subliminal. The more knowledge one has of Hmong culture, the more meanings the listener can find in the stories. The stories are a window into the Hmong's worldview.

Storytelling is still a vital tool for families and schools to use. The benefits of storytelling are broad and varied. Consider the following justifications for storytelling.

Storytelling provides a much-needed opportunity for listeners of all ages to interact on a very personal level. American society operates on an age-segregated model in schools, television, and movies. Storytelling, however, appeals to all and brings people together for a shared experience.

Storytelling develops an awareness of and sensitivity to the thoughts and feelings of the listeners. As the teller looks directly at the listeners, eyes and minds meet. The storyteller gets immediate feedback on how the story is being received, and the listeners gain added messages in the story from the paralinguistic actions of the storyteller. *Both* storyteller and listener are actively involved.

Storytelling stimulates the imagination and mental visualization. As the storyteller spins his or her magic, the listener creates pictures in his or her own mind of what the setting and characters look like and creates images of the story events. Every listener will "see" images that are unique and special.

Storytelling is an art form. It reflects all literatures and cultural archetypes for education, entertainment, and therapeutic purposes. Storytelling helps us see ourselves in a cosmological sense. The truths of the stories are about human existence and are intended to give meaning and value to peoples' experiences. In the words of a competent storyteller, we discover that we are all one community.

Storytelling enhances a child's education. One way it does this is through oral language. Our language comes alive when it is heard. Storytelling helps us remember the "shape" of stories. The more we hear stories, the more we learn story shapes. Storytelling also fosters a rich knowledge of literature, thereby broadening a child's choice of books and stories to read. Having an audience also helps the storyteller. As a person tells a story to others, he or she is more aware of what "works," what is needed, and what will catch the listeners' attention.

Telling a Story Successfully

All storytellers give one crucial piece of advice to would-be storytellers: Choose a story you like. That is probably one of the most important factors in telling a story successfully. If the story isn't one that you like, you'll have a hard time selling it to listeners—your lack of personal enjoyment of the story will show through.

Other things you can do to make the story work include learning the shape of the story. Don't memorize the story—that is a deadly beginning for a storyteller. Learn the shape of the story and then you will be able to add details to the bones to flesh it out. Many storytellers and story listeners can attest to the horrors of someone memorizing a story and then, in the middle of the presentation, forgetting details or what comes next.

It is important to practice telling the story. You can tell it to yourself, make an audio tape, practice in front of a mirror, or tell your story to family and friends. This practice will improve your success as a storyteller by helping you recognize where you need to make adjustments.

How do you evaluate your storytelling? Did you enter into the story with a ritual movement such as taking two steps forward before you began? Did you convey action and the sequence of events clearly? Were you able to assume the characters' point of view and express human motives, conflicts, and values? How did you establish the mood? Did you use figurative language, creative, or rhythmical language? Did you speak clearly, distinctly, and with varied intonation? Were your gestures appropriate? Did you use eye contact? Was the story ending a graceful one?

To complete our quick look at the art of storytelling, in the words of Isaac Bashevis Singer: "The future isn't here yet and you cannot foresee what it will bring. The present is only a moment and the past is one long story. Those who don't tell stories and don't hear stories live only for the moment and that isn't enough."

Stories are light-as-air, deep-as-breath, transforming heirlooms passed down with love, beauty, and form. Everyday stories by and about everyday people can also develop connections for us. Stories promote the understanding of traditional bonds between human beings and the natural world. They build awareness. Stories enchant us. That goes back to shaman beliefs in which the shaman enchants through chants and entrances the listener. Stories are catalogs of collective wisdom that are amusing, instructive, and important to our world view. They guide us in many ways.

One definition of the word *inspiration* is the act of drawing in a breath of air. The stories around us give us inspiration—ah ha!—as well as they inspire us—aaah! When we retell stories, we keep ourselves alive; they are our legacies. Stories give us images for what is truly worth seeking, worth having, worth doing. They help us dwell in place. The Hmong, Native Americans, and other peoples ground their stories in nearby fields, lakes, rivers, and mountains and carry their places in mind. This imaginative bond between person, place, and creature needs to be nourished.

The story "The Orphan Boy and His Wife" (*Folk Stories of the Hmong*, p. 108) was taken from a story cloth, one way the Hmong share their stories with the world. Because the Hmong did not have a written language until the 1950s, books weren't everyday items, but their other arts served as ways of telling their stories. Read this story and analyze it for the elements included in the activity section.

The Orphan Boy and His Wife

A long time ago, an old woman said to an orphan, "I'm sorry your mother and father are dead. You need a wife."

The orphan boy said, "I can't marry anyone. I don't have any clothes. I don't have a house. I don't have any money."

The old woman said, "You can marry a wife. Go sit by the road and watch. All kinds of people will come by. Some will be dressed very elegantly and look very nice. You should not bother with those people. When you see three sisters riding on thin, sickly, dirty horses with dry manure all over them, the one you want is the youngest sister, who will be riding on the last horse. Speak to the three sisters. You should grab the tail of the youngest sister's horse and never let go of it no matter what happens."

So the orphan sat by the road and watched. There were many people coming by on the road. Some were dressed in silk and silvery clothes and were very attractive. Then he saw three sisters riding dirty horses. He grabbed the last horse's tail and held on to it. Nia Ngao Zhua Pa looked at him and said, "Please let go of my horse's tail. I am in a hurry."

He didn't do as she asked. Her oldest sister said, "Nia Ngao Zhua Pa, why argue with this orphan? He may be the husband fortune sent to you."

Nia Ngao Zhua Pa tried to ruffle herself up to scare him, like a hen does with her feathers. He just said, "Oh, that doesn't scare me a bit."

After a while she went with him and she married him. First, Nia Ngao Zhua Pa took some leaves and changed them into a beautiful house. Then she took off her ring and changed it into a rice pot. Then she took off her bracelet and changed it into a stove. She took half a grain of rice. He thought it was too little. "How can it be enough for both of us to eat?" he asked.

"Don't worry," she said. "There will be plenty. If there is not enough, you may eat it all and I won't have any."

She changed it into a pot full of rice. Then she took a flower and changed it into a cooked chicken. The orphan was surprised and knew he had a good wife. He was happy and rich.

But after a long time of watching their happiness, a neighbor girl, Nia Ngao Kou Kaw, said, "The orphan and his wife are rich. I'm poor. I want to be rich, too."

She was jealous. She thought, "I will hurt the orphan's wife." Then she said to the orphan, "Your wife is a bad woman. She drank dragon's blood. She drank nine bowls of dragon's blood. Tell your wife to go away and I will marry you. I will be a good wife."

For three days the neighbor girl Nia Ngao Kou Kaw said to the orphan, "Your wife is a bad woman. I am beautiful. Tell your wife to go away. I will marry you."

So the orphan said to his wife, Nia Ngao Zhua Pa, "A beautiful young girl wants to marry me." Many days of this went on, and finally one day he told his wife to go away, but his wife didn't want to go away. She said, "I want to live with you." The orphan began to tell her regularly to go away.

"I want to marry a beautiful young girl. I don't want you here." So the orphan's wife went to the lake. She walked into it. She said, "Please, my husband, tell me to come back."

But the husband didn't say anything. The wife said, "Please, my husband. The water is up to my knees. Tell me to come back."

But the husband didn't say anything. The wife said, "Please, my husband. The water is up to my waist. Tell me to come back."

But the husband didn't say anything. The wife implored him, "Please, my husband. The water is up to my neck. Tell me to come back."

But the husband still didn't say anything. And then the water was over his wife's head. She was gone. The orphan went home, but his house was gone, and only leaves were in its place. He said, "Where is my beautiful house?" He married the neighbor girl, Nia Ngao Kou Kaw, but he was not happy. He took to regularly visiting the lake where his wife was. He sat down by the lake and he cried, "I want to see Nia Ngao Zhua Pa."

A frog that happened to be nearby heard him and said, "I can drink the water. I can drink all the water. Then you can see Nia Ngao Zhua Pa. But, don't laugh! You must not laugh."

So the frog drank and drank. He drank half the water and his stomach got very big. The orphan laughed, "Ha, ha, ha!" and the frog's stomach burst open, *poosh*!

The water went back into the lake—*swoosh*! The orphan looked at the lake. He said, "What can I do? I want to see Nia Ngao Zhua Pa. I want to tell her to come back! Who can help me? I know, I'll go to the shoa. He knows everything. He will tell me what to do." And so the orphan went to see the shoa.

The shoa gave him advice. "Go and beg the frog again. Sew his stomach back up."

The orphan did as he was instructed. He begged the frog to try again. The frog finally agreed. "Remember, you must not laugh. If you do I'll never do it again for you." So the orphan promised and sewed the frog's stomach back up. The frog drank and drank the water again, and this time the orphan didn't laugh.

When the water was gone he saw his wife at the bottom of the lake, making needlework, sewing beautiful *pa ndau*. He looked back at the frog, who looked ridiculous, and, forgetting his promise, he laughed. This time the frog was furious. "If you were really sad you wouldn't laugh at me no matter how silly I look. I am not going to help you again."

The orphan cried and cried and begged the frog, but the frog refused to drink the water. The orphan sadly dragged himself home. The next day he came back to the lake. He saw on the shore and cried, and cried, and cried. The frog wandered by and heard him crying.

The orphan saw the frog and started to beg him to drink the water. He begged, pleaded, and cried. The frog felt sorry for the orphan, so he drank the water again and this time the orphan didn't laugh. After a while he saw his wife at the bottom of the lake, and he jumped in with her. He grabbed her by the arm and spoke to her.

"You wanted to marry a young girl," she reminded him. "You have a black heart and are very bad. Why are you still following me?"

The orphan begged her to forgive him. He told her, "I had been tempted so many times I became weak. I am sorry. Please, please, please forgive me."

Finally she relented, and today they are living at the bottom of the lake—married forever.

✔ DISCUSSION AND ACTIVITIES

◆ The Hmong value industry, intelligence, courage, patience, family loyalty, respect for parents, fidelity to a promise, kindness to the weak and disadvantaged, honesty, and integrity. Ask the students to identify the virtues in this story. Which ones were broken?

◆ What are some of the generalizations apparent in this story? (An example might be: One must look behind the surface to find true worth.)

◆ Use this story to create a readers theatre. Including the narrator, how many characters will you need for speaking parts? After the students have finished writing the script, get them to share this readers theatre version with others.

◆ Have students create illustrations for this story. These pictures could then be compiled into a book, photographed, and used in a slide/tape presentation or a video.

◆ Before preparing this story with illustrations for a book, develop storyboards as a guide for the book. Ask students to help you identify the important events of the story. Discuss events that you can imagine or infer as a result of the story.

◆ Develop a puppet presentation for this story.

♦ "The Orphan Boy and His Wife" has the typical theme of a minority people who have felt the pressures of having little, if any, political identity and power. Read other stories from *Folk Stories of the Hmong*, and find other examples of the poor orphan who is trodden upon by the rich and mighty. Are there any stories in which he finally triumphs?

♦ This story would be a good choice for oral storytelling with others. Start a journal devoted to documenting the class's storytelling activities. Include programs, announcements, and other material on storytelling concerts, swaps, and events.

♦ Have students make storytelling booklets. Here is a list of words to put in it. Have them arrange the words in alphabetical order and write a definition for each.

folklore	fairy tale	bard	myth
tradition	legend	culture	troubadour
folklorist	hero	griot	tall tales
contemporary	heroine	ancestors	proverb
minstrel	ancient	epic	fable
anthropologist	yarn	ballad	poem
haiku	oral history	how/why stories	

♦ Encourage storytelling by having the students keep an album of stories they like to tell along with pictures of themselves telling stories. They can also use the album to keep notes about how the each storytelling went and any new story and storytelling ideas they have.

♦ Read "Bird Couple's Vow" from *Folk Stories of the Hmong* (pp. 64–66). Then read "Jack and the King's Girl" from the classic collection of *The Jack Tales* by Richard Chase. Discuss with the class how these stories are similar and how they are different. Set up a two-column chart. List under a column titled "Alike" what makes the stories alike, and list under a column titled "Different" the ways in which the stories are different.

♦ Have the students write an original Cinderella story using Hmong characters and settings.

♦ Sew pieces of cloth to illustrate a tale. Use colors, shapes, and stitches to fill in the story details. You will need a piece of cloth for the background, with medium-sized scraps of fabrics and threads of different colors, and a needle.

♦ Have everyone sit in a circle. Instruct someone to start a story. Then stop, point to someone else, and say, "And then what happened?" The second person must continue the story from the point where the first teller quit. The story can continue like this until someone officially ends it.

♦ A variation on the previous activity uses a long piece of yarn with unevenly spaced knots tied in it. Roll the yarn into a ball. Have the person starting the story hang on to the end of the yarn and pass the ball around the circle. As the yarn ball travels, the narrator of the story changes whenever someone gets a knot; that person then takes over in the story until the next knot comes up.

VARIATIONS ON A THEME

There are variants on the story of Cinderella found throughout the world. The Cinderella story first appeared in *The Miscellaneous Record of Yu Yang,* which dates from the T'ang Dynasty (A.D. 618–907). Since the oldest European version was found to be an Italian tale from 1634, it seems that Cinderella made her way to Europe from Asia. The Hmong version, "Ngao Nao and Shee Na," can be found on pages 93–100 in *Folk Stories of the Hmong.* This story was also illustrated on a *pa ndau.* Read this story.

There are even high-tech Cinderella stories being developed today. For instance, read the following story—Cinderella with a twist!

High-Tech Cinderella

Once upon a time, there was a beautiful hacker named Cinderella. She was really a whiz at programming. Cinderella had three wicked stepsisters, all of whom had fancy expensive computers but didn't even know how to write BASIC code. They were very mean to Cinderella.

One night, while her stepsisters were at their user group meeting, a fairy godmother appeared before Cinderella and offered to grant her a wish.

"I wish I had a 1.44 megabyte disk drive," gushed Cinderella, "so I could go to the user group meeting and show them my new software!"

Quick as a wink, the disk drive appeared. But Cinderella's fairy godmother pointed her finger and said sternly, "I must warn you, Cinderella. You have to leave by midnight, or all your disks will crash."

"That's cool, Fairy Godmother," said Cinderella. "It won't take me long to run a few demos."

So quick as a mouse, Cinderella copied all her new software programs onto a disk and went to the users group meeting.

Well, the user group was enthralled by Cinderella's incredible software. In all of the excitement, Cinderella lost track of the time.

As the hour was getting late, the president of the user group strolled over. When he got a load of Cinderella's programming, he fell in love.

"This is the most well-executed database I've ever seen," he said. "Will you marry me?"

At that instant, Cinderella glanced at her on-screen clock and noticed that it was 11:58:43. In a minute and seventeen seconds, all her software would crash! She gathered her disks and ran out the door, dropping one in her haste. The president of the user group was heartbroken.

The next day he went knocking door to door with the disk in hand, looking for the computer that it would run on. "When I find the computer that's compatible with the operating system on this disk, I will have found my true love!" he said.

Well, he walked all over town, but no computers could run the software. When he got to Cinderella's house, the three wicked stepsisters all clamored for his attention.

"Gimme that disk, you nerd!" yelled the first wicked stepsister.

But alas, the software would not run on any of their computers. Just as the president of the user group was about to leave, he noticed a young girl dressed in rags who was doing some word processing in the corner.

"What about her?" he asked. "Perhaps the disk will run on her computer!"

"Hahahahahaha!" laughed the stepsisters. "We just keep her around to do our typing."

But he gave the young girl the disk anyway, and lo and behold, it ran perfectly!

"I love you!" he exclaimed. "Marry me and I'll give you a hard disk drive and all the programming utilities you'll ever need!"

And they lived compatibly ever after.

"High-Tech Cinderella" was written by Dan Gutman. The story first appeared in *The Miami Herald* on September 30, 1988, under the title, "It's Cinderella Via Disk Drive." Reprinted with permission of *The Miami Herald*.

Bibliography of Cinderella Variants

Climo, Shirley. *The Egyptian Cinderella.* Illustrated by Ruth Heller. New York: Thomas Y. Crowell, 1989.
  In this version of Cinderella set in Egypt in the sixth century B.C., Rhodopis, a slave girl, eventually comes to be chosen by the Pharaoh to be his queen.

———. *The Korean Cinderella.* Illustrated by Ruth Heller. New York: HarperCollins, 1993.
  Pear Blossom, a stepchild, eventually is chosen by the magistrate to be his wife.

Goode, Diane. *Cinderella.* New York: Alfred A. Knopf, 1988.
  Goode translated the story of Charles Perrault. With the help of a fairy god-mother, a mistreated kitchen maid attends the palace ball on condition that she leave before midnight. This book also has a companion audio cassette narrated by Jessica Lange.

Hague, Michael. *Cinderella and Other Tales from Perrault.* New York: Henry Holt, 1989.
  Hague has illustrated eight stories with lavish, full-color pictures.

Hickox, Rebecca. *The Golden Sandal* (a Middle Eastern Cinderella story). Illustrated by Will Hillenbrand. New York: Holiday House, 1998.
  This story is based on a Cinderella story from Iraq called "The Little Red Fish and the Clog of Gold." A kind and beautiful girl is mistreated by her stepmother and step-sisters, but she finds a husband with the help of a magic fish.

Huck, Charlotte. *Princess Furball.* Illustrated by Anita Lobel. New York: Greenwillow, 1989.
  A princess in a coat of a thousand furs hides her identity from a king who falls in love with her.

Jackson, Ellen. *Cinder Edna.* Illustrated by Kevin O'Malley. New York: Lothrop, Lee & Shepard, 1994.
  Cinderella and Cinder Edna, who live with cruel stepmothers and stepsisters, have different approaches to life. Each ends up with the prince of her dreams, but one is a great deal happier than the other.

Lattimore, Deborah Nourse. *Cinderhazel* (the Cinderella of Halloween). New York: Scholastic, 1997.
  An untidy witch named Cinderhazel discovers that Prince Alarming likes dirt as much as she does.

Louie, Ai-Ling, trans. and reteller. *Yeh Shen.* Illustrated by Ed Young. New York: Philomel, 1982.
  Yeh Shen includes an ancient Chinese manuscript of the story. It is illustrated by Caldecott Award–winner Ed Young. Yeh-Shen's slippers were woven of golden threads in a pattern like scales of a fish and had glistening solid-gold soles.

Minters, Frances. *Cinder Elly*. Illustrated by G. Brian Karas. New York: Viking, 1994.
  This is a rap version of the traditional fairy tale. The overworked younger sister gets to go to a basketball game and meets a star player, Prince Charming.

✔ DISCUSSION AND ACTIVITIES

- Discuss the themes and events of "Ngao Nao and Shee Na."

- Ask the students to describe how this version compares or contrasts with others they know.

- Read some of the suggested picture-book versions of Cinderella (see Chapter 4, "Thoughts on Writing"). Develop a chart to compare and contrast the stories.

- Discuss why students think Cinderella stories are so popular and have traveled and survived for so long.

- Have your students create an African Cinderella story.

- Rewrite "Ngao Nao and Shee Na" into a readers theatre script to present to others.

TWO STORIES FROM TWO CULTURES

  As was mentioned earlier, stories have been used to explain how things should be, the way to behave properly, how things came to be, and how the world was created. They also serve to fulfill the wishes of people. What more can people wish for than health and enough food to keep hunger away? The following stories demonstrate these wishes. They also include another common folk story element— magical objects.
  One story, "The Taiga Sampo, or the Magic Mill," is from Finland (refer to other Finnish stories that include these same wishes, as well as the story of why the sea has salt in *The Enchanted Wood and Other Tales from Finland* by Norma and George Livo (Libraries Unlimited, 1999). The other story, "Zeej Choj Kim, the Lazy Man," is Hmong. Read them both.

The Taiga Sampo, or The Magic Mill

Vainamoinen, the oldest of the ancient Finnish wizards, had just had one of his most harrowing adventures with a vengeful enemy, Joukahainen, who had shot Vainamoinen's blue elk. Vainamoinen was aided by an eagle. Not a big one and yet not a small one. The eagle was of a size in which one wing grazed the water and the other swept the heavens. Its tail was in the sea, and it whetted its beak on the cliffs.

The eagle found Vainamoinen weak and tired, for even ancient wizards lost their lusty youth. The eagle told Vainamoinen to climb on him because in the past, Vainamoinen had cleared the trees of Kaleva so the fields could be burned, plowed, and seeded to grow crops. In doing this he left one lonely birch tree as a resting place for the birds. The eagle had remembered this. And so, on the wing tip of the eagle, Vainamoinen traveled along the path of the cold spring wind to the North Farm. Louhi, mistress of the north country, took him to her home and fed the weakened hero. She presented him with a feast of salmon and pork. She gave him a warm bath and rubbed life back into his muscles.

Vainamoinen was deeply depressed from his recent trials and tribulations and only wanted to be back in his own lands near his own sauna, listening to the songs of his own birds. He knew the North Farm was a place where other heroes told of people who ate each other and even drowned their own heroes.

"If you can forge a Sampo, beat out a lid of many colors from the tip of the shaft of a swan's feather, from the milk of a farrow cow, from a single barleycorn, from the fleece of a summer ewe, then I will give you my own daughter to marry and return you to your home," said Louhi.

Vainamoinen, weary and tired, told her, "I don't have the skill to do that, but my old brother Ilmarinen the craftsman can do it. He forged the heavens—beat out the firmament with such skill that there is no trace of a hammer or spot to show where his tongs gripped the heavens."

Louhi pledged, "I will give my daughter to whosoever forges me the Sampo. If you bring such a craftsman here, I will let you go to your home. You must keep this promise." Saying this, she harnessed a stallion to a huge sleigh and warned Vainamoinen, "Do not raise your head as you travel home or disaster and evil will overtake you."

As the sled traveled over the cold, frozen northland, Vainamoinen saw a dazzling maiden sitting on the edge of a rainbow, weaving cloth of gold and silver and spinning threads of gold and silver with a golden spindle. Not thinking of Louhi's warning, Vainamoinen stopped and spoke to the maiden. "You most beautiful of women, come home with me and be my wife. I am the eternal singer. You will live graciously with me."

The maiden gives him some impossible tasks to do, and Louhi's warning of disaster comes true. Through luck and help, though, Vainamoinen continues his trip home. He knew that he would have to trick Ilmarinen into forging the Sampo. As he drew near to the fields of Osmo, Vainamoinen sang up a bush-crowned birch tree. It was crowned with golden leaves that rose through the clouds to the heavens with its foliage spreading in all directions. He sang for a moon to gleam in the gold-crowned tree and put the stars of the Great Bear in its branches. Satisfied that this would tempt Ilmarinen, he went straight to the blacksmith shop of Ilmarinen.

"Ho, Vainamoinen. You have been gone a long time," Ilmarinen greeted him. "Where have you been and what mighty things have you done?"

Vainamoinen replied, "I have been staying in the gloomy North Farm, skiing about on Lappish skis in the land of the north magicians. There are many amazing things to see there. If you can forge a Sampo with a lid of many colors, you can win the comely maiden of the North Farm, daughter of Louhi. Many pursue her, but she will have none of them. With the Sampo, she would be yours."

Ilmarinen became suspicious. "Vainamoinen, old stout-hearted singer, I fear you have promised that I would create a Sampo as ransom for your freedom. Can this be?"

"Dear brother Ilmarinen, the things I tell you are true. The North Farm is full of marvels, and I brought one of them back with me. Come see it." Saying this Vainamoinen led Ilmarinen to the tree crowned with golden leaves, the moon in the crown of the leaves, and the Great Bear sparkling on its branches.

"It truly is a marvel," agreed Ilmarinen.

"Look to the heights at the moon. Even you could climb up there and gather the moon in your arms as a prize," said Vainamoinen.

At this idea, Ilmarinen quickly threw off his blacksmith apron and started to climb the tree. "While I am up there, I will get the Great Bear too." He climbed higher and higher into the gleaming tree, and then Vainamoinen sang the winds to a fury to carry Ilmarinen to the North Farm. The winds carried the tree and Ilmarinen over the moon, under the sun, and on the shoulders of the Great Bear. They dropped him in one of Louhi's fields. Her dogs just stood there amazed. Louhi came outside to see what the winds were about and saw Ilmarinen.

"Come into my house," she said. "You must be the greatest of craftsmen I have heard about." As she came into the house with him, she went upstairs and told her daughter to dress in her best gown made of gold, silver, and copper.

When the maiden of the North appeared in her incredible dress, Ilmarinen could not take his eyes off of her. She was lovelier than Vainamoinen had told him. He must have her for his wife. And so he agreed to make the Sampo.

He had to build a forge and begin from the beginning. After he added the tip of the shaft of a swan's feather, the milk of a farrow cow, the tiny ear of barley, and the fleece of a summer ewe to the furnace, he saw things forming. But Louhi said of the gold, "These nuggets are just children's playthings." Of the silver objects she announced, "These are just a horse's jingling bells. Make me a Sampo."

And so for seven days he broke and returned to the furnace things that appeared until he finally saw the Sampo being born. He skillfully lifted it out and gourged a grain mill on one side, a salt mill on a second, and a money mill on the third side. He formed a lid of many colors that spun around and held a bin of things to eat, a bin for things to sell, and a bin for household supplies.

Louhi was delighted. The North Country would never be poor or hungry again. She took the Sampo to a special place for safekeeping. It was placed inside a hill of rock, inside the copper mountain, behind nine doors with locks. It grew three roots nine fathoms deep. One root went into solid rock, a second into the sea shore, and the third into the earth near Louhi's house.

"Ilmarinen smiled, "Now that the Sampo is done, I will take my beautiful bride and return to my own land."

"Ah, wonderful creator of the Sampo," started the daughter, "I do not have the time to leave here. The land and the birds need me. Besides, I am not ready to marry."

Ilmarinen could tell that there was no way to persuade her to change her mind. Downcast, he only wanted to go home. Louhi conjured a craft with a copper paddle. "This ship will be a gentler way to travel on the gales of the north wind than a tree was. Use it to make your way home."

Much time and many adventures and wives later, Vainamoinen and Ilmarinen were talking of how bad things were in their homeland now. Crops died. Coldness came, and the people suffered. "While we are in bad times, the people living at the North Farm are in the midst of plenty because of the Sampo," complained Ilmarinen. "They have things to eat, sell, and store in their homes. There is plowing, sowing, and all sorts of increase and everlasting good fortune in Pohja. All from the Sampo I made."

Vainamoinen decided that they needed to share the riches of the Sampo. "Let us go north and get part of the Sampo for our needs."

That would be impossible," warned Ilmarinen. "The Sampo is in a hill of rock inside the copper mountain, behind nine doors with huge locks, and with enormous roots."

Vainamoinen finally convinced Ilmarinen that it was the only thing they could do. So they set out by boat for the North Farm. When they got there they told Louhi that they needed to share the Sampo and the lid of many colors.

"The Sampo is mine alone," screamed Louhi. "It is mine!"

The eternal sage Vainamoinen said, "If you won't share with us, we will have to take it all." With that, he took out his *kantele,* a harp made from a pike's jawbone, and played and sang such marvelous music that the people of the North Farm fell asleep. While they were sleeping, he sang the nine solid doors open into the mountain of copper. Vainamoinen and Ilmarinen got Louhi's steer to plow and pull up the roots of the Sampo. They took the Sampo to their boat for the trip to the end of the foggy island at the tip of the misty headland to a space never visited by humankind.

However, a young, romantic, headstrong fellow who had traveled with them on this adventure started to sing a boastful song of victory. This reckless youth's raspy, roaring, quavering voice frightened a crane who flew off. The crane flew over Louhi's house, squawking loudly and waking Louhi from her sleep.

Louhi discovered that the Sampo was missing. She beseeched the spirit of the mist to help her stop Vainamoinen and Ilmarinen. She evoked fog, gales, and a malevolent sea spirit to help her. The trials of the heroes were fought by Vainamoinen with magic songs of his own. The pikebone harp was lost overboard in a storm, but that is another story.

Louhi conjured a warship with thousands of archers and men with spears. When Vainamoinen sang its ruin, she gathered the splinters of wood from the boat and made herself into an eagle. She flew to their ship, but Vainamoinen defeated her again. With only the part of one talon left, Louhi seized the Sampo and threw it into the sea where it and the lid broke into pieces. With the Sampo sinking to the bottom of the sea, the waters would never again lack for treasures, and of course, the grinding of the salt mill explains why the seas have salt.

In misery, Louhi set out for home. Her prestige was gone, and she had been defeated, and that was why there was poverty at Pohja.

After Louhi was vanquished, Vainamoinen had Ilmarinen forge an iron rake with close-set teeth and a long handle so he could rake the billows to get his *kantele* back. With it he raked up water lilies, shore rubbish, bits of sedge, and the litter of rushes, but he could not find his pikebone harp. However, he was able to go ashore and gather pieces of the Sampo and its lid to take them to the tip of the misty headland at the end of the foggy island. He planted the Sampo pieces in the earth, and with charms he was able to make these pieces of the Sampo grow. The land became rich in barley and rye. This brought joy to Vainamoinen once again.

Zeej Choj Kim, the Lazy Man

A long time ago, there was a man named Zeej Choj Kim. He lived with an emperor who had two sons and a daughter named Ntxawm. Zeej Choj Kim was very lazy and spent most of his time sleeping.

The emperor's sons liked to go fishing a lot. Coming home from one of their fishing trips, they accidentally dropped a fish on the trail.

Zeej Choj Kim found this fish. Being very hungry, he picked the fish up to cook it for himself. The fish was quite dirty, so he decided to wash it before he cooked it. But Zeej Choj Kim was so lazy that he did not want to carry water from the stream to wash the fish. Instead, he washed the fish by urinating on it.

He cooked the fish in a fire pit. When the fish was almost ready to eat, Ntxawm, the emperor's daughter and her family happened by and saw and smelled the fish cooking. She wanted to eat some of the fish. All of her relatives told her not to eat the fish, but she insisted.

After Ntxawm ate the fish, she became pregnant. Her father, the emperor, accused her of mating with Zeej Choj Kim, but she denied it. The emperor then went to Zeej Choj Kim and accused the lazy man of mating with his daughter. Of course, Zeej Choj Kim protested loud and long and said he was innocent.

The emperor did not quite know what to do about all of this. "If you two insist that you have not mated with each other, then I will have to wait until the baby is born. After that, we will take the child to look for his or her father."

When the baby was born, it was a sturdy boy. The emperor took the baby to every single man in town and gave each one the baby to hold. He decreed that if the baby did not cry, then that man must be the boy's father. But the baby always cried when each of the men held him. Finally, Zeej Choj Kim was told to hold the baby, and the baby did not cry, but smiled and gurgled happily.

The emperor was furious. He scolded his daughter. He raged. He told Ntxawm that she was no good. He asked, "Why did you mate with such a lazy man?"

In anger, he ordered his sons, "Take Zeej Choj Kim and Ntxawm to the river and kill them!"

The royal sons had no choice but to obey their father. As they walked to the river, one of the brothers said, "I do not want to kill Zeej Choj Kim. Remember when we built our house a few years ago and we asked all the people in town to come and help us quarry and carry stones? It took a lot of time, and even then, we never had enough stones to build the house. But when Zeej Choj Kim chiseled the stones, he was so strong that the stones broke easily, just like dry corn. And the stones he carried in only one trip were more than enough for us to build the house. I suggest we do not kill him."

The other brother agreed. Instead, they walked Zeej Choj Kim and Ntxawm to the river and left them there.

The couple stayed at the riverside. They had no food and Zeej Choj Kim was so lazy that he did not want to go hunting. He just laid himself on the sand and did not move. He looked like he was dead. Two crows, one white and the other black, flew overhead and saw him. They thought he was dead, so the white crow flew down and landed on Zeej Choj Kim's stomach. The crow was just getting ready to eat him when Zeej Choj Kim grabbed the crow's feet and yelled to Ntxawm, "I have caught a crow. We'll kill him and have dinner."

The white crow cried and begged to be set free, but Zeej Choj Kim insisted that he was too hungry to wait any longer. "You are dinner," he said to the crow.

The crow pleaded, "If you let me go, I will give you my magic ball."

"I want the ball first before I will let you go," replied Zeej Choj Kim.

The white crow called to the black crow, which was still flying overhead. "Go and bring my magic ball and give it to this man so he will set me free."

The black crow heard and flew away. But when the black crow came back, he asked, "White crow, should I bring the one that has one chamber or the one that has three chambers?"

"Bring the one that has one chamber and save the one with three chambers," was the reply.

"Oh no," said Zeej Choj Kim. "If you bring the one with three chambers, then I will let you go. If not, I will kill you."

The white crow cried, "Black crow, bring the one that has three chambers."

In a little while the black crow returned again. "White crow, should I bring the one that has three chambers or the one with five chambers?" he asked.

The answer came, "Bring the one with three chambers and save the one with five chambers."

"Zeej Choj Kim demanded, "Oh, no! If you bring the one with five chambers, I will set you free. Otherwise, I will eat you for dinner!"

"Bring the one with five chambers and save the one with three chambers," called the white crow.

The black crow flew away. He came back shortly and asked again, "White crow, should I bring the one that has five chambers or the one with seven chambers?"

Quickly, the white crow replied, "Bring the one with five chambers and save the other one."

Zeej Choj Kim called to Ntxawm, "Begin to boil water. We will have to kill the crow to eat if he does not want to give us the magic ball with the seven chambers."

The white crow whined, "Don't start to boil the water yet. I will give you the one with seven chambers," and he instructed the black crow to hurry and bring it back.

Once more the black crow disappeared. When he came back he asked, "White crow, should I bring the one that has seven chambers or the one with nine?"

"Bring the one with seven and save the one with nine," said the white crow.

Zeej Choj Kim repeated what he had said before, so the white crow again changed his mind. "Bring the ball with nine chambers."

Finally, the black crow returned with the magic ball with nine chambers and gave it to Zeej Choj Kim. "Now that you have the magic ball, let me go," demanded the white crow.

"First, you must show me how it works. Then I will set you free," was the answer.

The white crow explained how to use the ball. "The first chamber is chicken. The second is pork, the third is beef, the fourth is vegetables, the fifth is rice, the sixth is mushrooms, the seventh is fruit, the eighth is water, and the ninth chamber is wine. When you want to eat or drink something you just say, "Daa daa chi fa, daw daw chi dhau." Then it will cook what you want."

"Tell it to cook some food for me before I let you go," demanded Zeej Choj Kim.

The white crow chanted, "Daa daa chi fa, daw daw chi dhau." A meal appeared. It was the most delicious food that Zeej Choj Kim and Ntxawm had ever eaten. Zeej Choj Kim let the white crow go. Now, they never had to worry about being hungry.

Meanwhile, the emperor was fighting a war. His soldiers fought for many days, but they kept losing ground. One of the emperor's sons said, "Father, perhaps we should call our brother-in-law Zeej Choj Kim to come and help us."

The emperor roared, "I thought you killed him a long time ago. Did you not kill him when I ordered you to?"

"No, Father. We did not kill him," the son said softly.

"Well, I don't think he really could help us. Why even bother to call him—he is such a lazy man," mused the emperor.

The second son interrupted. "But, father, it never hurts to call for help. If he can't help us then at least we can say we did our best."

Finally, after much argument, the emperor agreed. The sons ran down to the river to search for Zeej Choj Kim and Ntxawm. They found the couple and asked for help in the fight. Zeej Choj Kim agreed to help. "But first, you must go home and kill nine bulls and cook nine giant woks full of meat and bring nine giant hollowed-out wooden steamers of rice for me to eat. Then I will be ready to fight."

When the emperor saw his sons return he asked, "So, will your strong brother-in-law help us?"

They told their father what Zeej Choj Kim had told them to do. The emperor laughed crazily and snorted, "I bet your brother-in-law won't be able to eat all that food. Neither will he help us fight."

The two sons ignored their father and did as Zeej Choj Kim had told them.

Finally, Zeej Choj Kim came. He had a bag with him. In the bag was the magic ball. After he arrived, he opened the bag and set the ball on the ground. Soldiers began to come out of the ball. There were hundreds and thousands of them. The first soldiers out of the ball ate and had already gone to fight when the next soldiers walked out of the ball. They, too, ate and then left to fight. Before the last group of soldiers had even finished eating, the first group had already won the battle.

When the emperor arrived at the battlefield, only three soldiers remained. He was very pleased and said, "Save those three to carry salt for us! My son-in-law, my real son-in-law, my amazing son-in-law, you have done a marvelous thing. Please come back with us and we will celebrated our victory."

Zeej Choj Kim and Ntxawm were invited to come back to live in town with the emperor and his sons. People paid respect to them, and they all lived happily ever after.

From "Zeej Choj Kim, the Lazy Man." In *Folk Stories of the Hmong: Peoples of Laos, Thailand, and Vietnam*. Englewood, CO: Libraries Unlimited, 1991. Reprinted by permission.

✔ DISCUSSION AND ACTIVITIES

♦ Ask students to discuss why they think these two stories were created. What needs of people are common to all of us?

♦ As the class discusses how these stories are alike and different, write two lists in which you compare and contrast the stories.

♦ Ask students to identify some of the cultural details of the stories.

♦ Have students write a modern-day story like these set in the United States. Brainstorm ideas for characters, needs of the people, problems, and magical objects.

♦ Encourage students to share their stories with a partner. Were there things that your partner didn't understand? Were there things about their story that they felt were special?

♦ Once the stories have been written, students will enjoy illustrating them. Refer to the suggestions for using various art media (pp. 59–60).

Every culture has stories of love and ghosts. The following story is a combination of both of these themes.

Love Ghost Story

A long time ago, there was a young Hmong man and woman who loved each other very much. They lived in separate villages. The young woman's village was just a single household. The young man visited his girlfriend in her village almost every day, for they were so much in love.

Even though they loved each other very much, their parents didn't allow them to marry. One day, the young man went to farm in his family's faraway field. He had been gone for a few days, and during that time his girlfriend became very sick and died. He returned home and told his parents that he wanted to go visit his girlfriend in her village.

His parents told him that while he was gone his girlfriend became sick and died. They told him not to go to visit her because she was dead. He didn't believe them. He loved and missed his girlfriend so much he determined to go and see for himself. He did not believe that she could have died so quickly.

It was almost dark when he arrived at the edge of his girlfriend's village. He picked a piece of banana leaf and blew a musical melody that he always played to call his girlfriend. Usually when she heard this leaf-blowing music, she dressed very nicely and went to sit outside on the porch, combing her hair and waiting for him. There she was on the porch. She gestured to him to come but he replied that it wasn't totally dark yet and he was too shy to come to her. "Let's wait until it is dark and then I will come," he said. The girl returned to her house to wait for him.

When it was dark he came to his girlfriend's house and she was sitting by the fire pit in the dark. She had not started a fire, and the house was dark. He couldn't see anything. "You should start a fire," he told her.

"You start it. I am very shy," she replied.

"It is not my home. I am actually more shy than you. It is your house. You should start the fire," he answered.

She started to light the fire in the fire pit. The first time she started to blow on the firewood, the fire did not start, so he could not see her face at all.

He urged her to continue to blow on the fire. Then she tried again and this time, he saw her face briefly. She looked very strange to him and he began to suspect something.

"Blow the on fire again," he told his girlfriend.

She was very reluctant to do this, but he kept begging her. She continued to blow on the firewood until the fire was fully bright enough to light up the house. He saw her face fully. It was swollen and looked ghastly. She was dressed in burial clothes—wearing a white skirt and long red and green sashes that were dotted with blood all over. She smelled of decay (*lwj*). He saw that the funeral drum and a reed instrument pipe (*keng*) was still hanging in the middle of the room. The corpse "horse," a parallel bamboo structure that holds the corpse, was still hanging along the back wall. It looked like she just got up from the corpse horse to sit down by the fire pit. There was no one else around.

After he glanced around the house, a chill traveled all over his body and he began to shake. He became very afraid. He asked with a quiver in his voice, "Where are your parents?"

"Oh, they went to work in the field," she answered. The truth of the matter was that they had actually run away during the middle of her funeral.

Her parents and their relatives were performing funeral rituals for her in the middle of the night after she had been dead for three days. Her body had already begun to decay, but she opened her eyes very wide and began to move her body as if she would get up and chase after them.

Her parents and all of the funeral attendees were so afraid that they all ran away. Of course her boyfriend did not know all of this had happened. Slowly, finally, he realized that she had become a ghost.

"Let me go outside of the house. I need to pee," he begged.

She quietly told him, "Oh, you can pee inside this house. You don't need to go outside to do it."

"I am shy and since we are only boyfriend and girlfriend I am uncomfortable doing that," he replied. "Please just let me go outside."

She thought for a moment and said, "Well, if you insist on going outside to pee, then let me tie my sashes on your waist to make sure you don't run away afterward."

He let her tie her sashes on his waist. As he walked out of the house he called, "When I have finished I will call you to pull the sashes. If you don't hear me call, don't pull on the sashes, I might not be finished."

When he got outside of the house, he tied the sashes on a house pole and ran away as fast as he could. She continued to wait, not knowing he was running away. She waited for a long time but he didn't call her. She called to him three times and there was no answer. She suddenly realized that he had probably run away. She began to pull her sashes, but she could not pull them back. They were tied tightly. She went outside and found that he had tied her sashes around the pole of the house. She was really angry and suddenly changed herself into a ghost and started to chase after him.

He had just entered a house in the neighboring Khumu tribe when she arrived at the edge of the same village. As he entered the house, he was shaking all over and was unable to say a word. He just fell down in the middle of the common room floor.

The owner of the house realized that he must be in some big trouble, so he placed a huge wine steamer over him. The owner waited by the door.

The ghostly girlfriend had changed herself into a beautiful woman as she entered the village looking for her boyfriend. She tracked his footprints to the house where he was hiding. When she arrived at the door she asked the owner, "Have you seen my boyfriend?"

"No, I have not," answered the owner.

"But I have followed his footprints to your house," she stated firmly.

"We have footprints also. Your boyfriend isn't the only one who has them. He is not here," the owner emphatically announced.

After the owner had told her that, she walked down the village. When she came to the edge of the village she changed herself into a ghost again. All the dogs of the village chased after.

Back at the house, the owner removed the wine steamer from the young man and sent him home by taking the path up the village. When the young man arrived back at home, he suddenly became sick for several days and then he too, died.

✔ DISCUSSION AND ACTIVITIES

- Have students go to the library to find other ghost stories. Share them in class.

- When do people usually tell ghost stories to others? What ghost stories do your students remember hearing when they were younger? Were they frightened by them? Did they tell them to others?

- Ask a librarian to help you find the Chinese story that is behind the Blue Willow dish pattern. It also is a love story that deals with death and transformation.

- Investigate, with a librarian, if ghost stories are checked out frequently.

4

Writing and
Illustrating Stories

THOUGHTS ON WRITING

Researchers have discovered that writing is good for what ails you. Although putting pen to paper won't cure schizophrenia or heart disease, studies show that writing about your deepest thoughts and feelings may help alleviate depression, prevent colds, boost your immune system and bolster the psyche.

Writing is also a wonderful way to discover things. If you let yourself write freely, it will take you places you have never imagined. You might wish to consider using a web, cluster, list, story map, or any other tool to help you organize your writing. Use your five senses: What does it look like? What are the smells? What do you hear? What do you feel physically and emotionally? What tastes might there be?

Figure 4.1 lists the elements that are basic to a good story. These elements may give you some direction in your writing.

✔ DISCUSSION AND ACTIVITIES

◆ Refer back to the story of Ngao Nao in *Folk Stories of the Hmong* (pp. 93–100). Have students write another Cinderella story. What specific regional artifacts and scenes would be appropriate?

◆ Instruct students to rewrite *Ngao Nao and Shee Na* in another writing genre, for instance, informational, poetry, rap, or science fiction.

Fig. 4.1. Elements of a story.

- Develop a storyboard of words and pictures to help students organize the events of Ngao Nao. The storyboard activity will help to identify and standardize details and sequence. These storyboard ideas, scenes, and events can be interchanged and evaluated for logical and effective structure.

- After the students have written their versions of Cinderella, have them create pictures. Their pictures can even be photographed with slide film and used as a slide/tape presentation of the story.

- Students might also enjoy creating a presentation using a video camera to record the art and text of their stories.

- Another way to present the Cinderella stories would be to create puppets and a puppet stage. The puppet show could be presented to community groups, schools, libraries, or bookstores.

- Have the students use the Ngao Nao story or their own Cinderella variant and create a readers theatre script.

ILLUSTRATING STORIES

Read the stories in *Folk Stories of the Hmong*. Choose one story to adapt and illustrate as a picture book or storybook. Many Hmong illustrations use stitchery and batik as their media (see figures 4.2, 4.3, and 4.4). Try out a number of art techniques using your own impressions of the story. Consider the following possibilities for the illustrations. Remember, you can mix the media for your illustrations.

Fig. 4.2. Scene from a folktale showing the wife stitching *pa ndau* while her husband is on the rock above as he comes to rescue her from the tigers.

Fig. 4.3. A couple going to gather firewood.

Fig. 4.4. A family on a trail with the baby being carried in the baby carrier on the woman's back.

Paper Cutting

The sharp contrast of black and white paper is eye-catching. Use scraps of paper and experiment with different shapes and colors. How can you build images using these elements? Refer to books by Gerald McDermott or Leo Lionni for examples of paper cutting.

Paper Weaving

Weave differently colored strips of paper into a variety of patterns. What textures can you create?

Tissue Paper

Cut tissue paper into very thin strips and then arrange them on paper covered with glue (such as Elmer's glue). Tissue paper makes a good material for collage work. Overlap the tissues and gradations of tone will appear. This technique is particularly appealing when you use tissue paper of a variety of colors.

Tracing Paper

You can create illustrations with a repeated pattern using tracing paper. These patterns can be used as borders.

Stenciling

Acetate or transparent material makes good stencils. Use sharp blades to cut the acetate. This technique is intended for use by older children under strict supervision.

Simpler stencils can be made from any fairly stiff card or paper using scissors, hole punches, or simply by tearing. Experiment with stencil designs.

Rubbings

Use a wax crayon to rub over paper or other light material that has been placed over a surface or object. Many surfaces and objects can be used for these rubbings, including floorboards, rocks, coins, and other items.

Finger Printing

Use washable paint or ink with any number of fingers or hands. Press fingers or hands on paints, and then press them onto paper. The prints can be cut up and rearranged into any design you desire.

String Block Printing

Select a piece of wood of any shape or size and cover one surface of it with glue. Choose any type of string for the block print—thick, thin, smooth, or coarse. Press the string onto the wood surface in any chosen pattern. The string can be moved about while the glue is still wet.

When the glue and string are dry, the surface will easily absorb ink. You can either apply the printing ink with a sponge or use a pad dipped into some ink in a dish. Press the block into it and then press the block onto paper or cloth for your print.

Polystyrene Printing

Polystyrene can be bought in sheets from craft suppliers or salvaged from packing. It can be incised with a pen point or fingernail. Apply the block printing ink with a sponge or brush to the polystyrene and press onto paper. The printed paper can also be cut into shapes to suit the illustration.

Wood Block Printing

For some interesting effects, apply ink to the ends of sawed wood. Another possibility is to chisel the grain of the wood block and print it onto paper. Again, the printed paper can be cut up into shapes to suggest images.

Using Other Objects

Leaves, shells, feathers, fabrics and other textured objects can be used in illustrations. Use an old toothbrush and poster paint to splatter paint over leaves and shapes. (Yarrow leaves make a particularly interesting design.) Combine these techniques and invent your own ideas or inspiration for your illustrations.

Making a Picture Book

Using your illustrations, create your own picture book from one of the stories in *Folk Stories of the Hmong*. Add a binding to your pages of art and adapted text. These books can be placed in your personal or a classroom library.

5

Hmong Folk Arts

Among Hmong folk arts are jewelry, clothing, *pa ndau*, and other forms of stitchery.

PA NDAU

For centuries, it has been a tradition among Hmong highlanders to celebrate births, marriages, and other events with gifts of squares of elaborate hand stitching. When enough of these squares were accumulated, they were sewn together on larger pieces of stitchery called *pa ndau*. Before 1965, *pa ndau* were used mainly to embellish Hmong clothing. Very thin needles, about one inch in length, were used for the stitching, which was usually done on cotton material. Between 1965 and 1975, *pa ndau* artists began incorporating new designs and colors in their work in order to sell their work to foreigners.

Pa ndau art incorporates appliqué, reverse appliqué, cross stitches, chain stitches, batik, and embroidery. Hmong needlework represents a changing record of a people's history and culture and thus provides priceless information. Embroidered "story cloths" make direct reference to Hmong myths, personal family history, animals and village life, war and death, disturbances associated with emigration, and life in a new land. Many story cloths originate in the former resettlement camps of Thailand and are sent to relatives living in the United States. No two pieces of *pa ndau* are exactly alike, because Hmong needlework is constantly changing and the people's artistic originality allows a continued expansion of their art.

Pa Ndau Samples

The colored pictures found on pages 17–32 of *Folk Stories of the Hmong* contain many samples of *pa ndau* stitchery on the clothing, background hanging, and story-cloths. Study these examples and see what you can discover.

✔ DISCUSSION AND ACTIVITIES

◆ Refer to Plate 35 on page 32 of *Folk Stories of the Hmong*. This *pa ndau* illustrates the natural environment, wild animals, and mystical creatures that are native to Laos. Have students draw a sketch of the plants, animals, and fantastic creatures that would be found in your own environment.

◆ Ask the students to identify and list as many fish, birds, amphibians, animals, and plants on this *pa ndau* as they can.

◆ Locate Laos on a globe. Measure how far (in miles) the country of Laos is from your state.

◆ Sometimes, for the sake of humor, a *pa ndau* will include animals that are not native to Laos. Ask students to identify any creature on this *pa ndau* that does not belong in Laos. Encourage them to consult an encyclopedia to discover what the climate is like in Laos.

◆ Plate 32 on page 31 in *Folk Stories of the Hmong* illustrates a folktale that begins on page 112. With this example in mind, have your students—individually or as a class—use the figures found in Plates 30 and 31 (p. 30) to write an original folk story of their own.

◆ Challenge students to make stitchery pictures of themselves, using colored thread and plain cotton cloth. What kind of pictures can they make? It might be helpful for them to lightly draw their pictures on the cloth with pencil as a guide for their stitches.

◆ Hmong textile art also includes weaving. Find out all you can about weaving. Are there any people in your area who are weavers? If so, arrange to have them present their art to your group.

◆ The Hmong used indigo as a dye for much of their textile art. Investigate other natural plants and minerals that are used as dye. Experiment dying fabric with them.

STRING-TYING CEREMONY

In Hmong culture, every newborn child's wrists are tied with cotton strings by an elderly villager. The strings are thought to protect the baby from misfortune and misery. As the strings are tied to each wrist, blessings are given. The following blessing is an example of what is traditional:

Blessing

I tie you with this string,
The life string,
The immortal string.
May you have merit,
May you grow tall and grow fast,
May you be physically strong and quick to learn.
If you look for silver,
May you get it.
If you look for gold,
May you get it.
May these strings protect you from all sickness.

The Hmong adopted another practice in Laos that also involves string-tying. It is called *baci* (figure 5.1). This ceremony is used during celebrations, such as graduations or weddings, whereby each person ties a string around the wrist of the person being celebrated. As they tie the string around the wrist, they also offer a blessing. Two such blessings are: *May your life be white as rice and clear as water* and *May you live 120 years*.

Fig. 5.1. *Baci*, or string-tying ceremony.

Shortly after the Hmong immigrated to the United States, friendship bracelets became the rage for young people. Kids had brightly colored bracelets knotted and braided from thread. One young girl told me, "You give these to your friends. It is one way of telling them you want them to be your friend for a long time."

Although the bracelets can be made with any fiber, embroidery floss seems to have been the most popular. Many commercial thread companies offered free how-to pamphlets and instruction sheets on how to make friendship bracelets.

It is also an interesting fact that the Mohawk Indians used to tie a leather thong around each person's wrist when they gathered for storytelling. This was done to keep the person's spirit safe in their body as the stories were told.

✔ DISCUSSION AND ACTIVITIES

♦ Create a list of blessings to be used at a string-tying ceremony. Would these blessings vary according to the occasion? If so, how and why?

♦ Have the students conduct interviews with their family members and their friends to see if any of them ever made and wore friendship bracelets. Discuss their discoveries as a class.

♦ For a great art activity, invite students to make a bracelet for a friend (see figure 5.2). What special blessing will they offer as they give their friends the bracelets?

JEWELRY

Silverworking is one of the tribal traditions of the Hmong. The silver jewelry is usually made by the men. The traditional necklace, worn for special occasions, contains lock-shaped pendants suspended by heavy chains from neck rings. Folklore tells us that during the times when the Hmong were enslaved by the Chinese, slaves were forced to wear large circular locks around their necks for identification. After they won their independence, the Hmong designed the necklaces in remembrance of the hardships of slavery. During the Vietnam War, the silver traditionally used for these necklaces became scarce. The Hmong then fashioned their necklaces using aluminum from downed planes.

✔ DISCUSSION AND ACTIVITIES

♦ Cut colored paper into one-inch squares. Have the students place a toothpick on one of the corners of paper, and roll the paper around the toothpick to form a tube. Once the tube is formed, the toothpick can be removed. They can then string the tubes (of different colors and sizes) into elaborate necklaces.

♦ Cut aluminum foil into pieces. Have the students fold, roll, and shape them into jewelry.

DMC® Friendship Bracelet Instructions

Now you're ready to make your Friendship Bracelet — it's quick and easy to do — and even more fun to wear!

What You'll Need
- DMC EMBROIDERY FLOSS (Article 117): 3 skeins in colors of your choice (the bracelet pictured on the front was made with light, medium and dark shades of a color). For instructional purposes, the 3 colors will be referred to as follows:
    - Color A — lightest shade
    - Color B — medium shade
    - Color C — darkest shade
- Tape or safety pin to hold strands of Floss while working.

To begin, cut 4 one-yard strands of Color A, 2 one-yard strands of Color B and 2 one-yard strands of Color C.

The width of your Bracelet is determined by the number of strands of Embroidery Floss used. The eight strands recommended in these instructions will result in a Friendship Bracelet approximately 3/8" wide.

Arrange the strands in the color order in which they will appear in your finished Friendship Bracelet. The color order for this Bracelet is 2 strands of Color A (A1, A2), 2 strands of Color B (B1, B2), 2 strands of Color A (A3, A4), 2 strands of Color C (C1, C2). Tie the eight strands together with a knot, leaving a 2 - 2½" tail (see Diagram 1).

Diagram 1

Using either tape or a safety pin, secure tail to a surface so that strands will be held in place while you work. You can tape it to a table or chair or pin it through the knot to your jeans. Smooth out the strands so that they are again in the correct color order.

The Knotting Technique
To begin, pick up strand A1 and wrap it over and under strand A2 to form a knot (see Diagram 2). Holding strand A2 taut, pull strand A1 until knot is tightened at top (see Diagram 3).

Now make a second knot, again wrapping strand A1 over and under strand A2 (see Diagram 4). Again, tighten knot by holding strand A2 taut while pulling strand A1 to the top. A double knot is now completed. Drop strand A2.

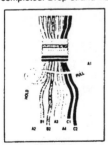
Diagram 2

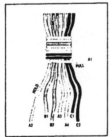
Diagram 3

Pick up strand B1 and wrap strand A1 over and under strand B1 (see Diagram 5). Tighten knot. Make second knot with strand A1 around strand B1. Drop strand B1.

Continue making knots in same manner across row, working strand A1 in a double knot around strands B2. A3, A4, C1 and C2. Strand A1 will be at far right side of row when all double

knots are completed. You will notice that this first row of double knots slants diagonally down towards the right (see Diagram 6).

For second row, use strand A2 to work same double knot over strands B1, B2, A3, A4, C1, C2 and A1. Strand A2 will now be at far right side of row next to strand A1.

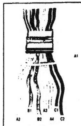
Diagram 4

Diagram 5

Diagram 6

Continue working rows in this manner:

Third Row: Work strand B1 over strands B2, A3, A4, C1, C2. A1 and A2.

Fourth Row: Work strand B2 over strands A3, A4, C1, C2, A1, A2 and B1.

Fifth Row: Work strand A3 over strands A4, C1, C2, A1, A2, B1 and B2.

Sixth Row: Work strand A4 over strands C1, C2, A1, A2, B1, B2 and A3.

Seventh Row: Work strand C1 over strands C2, A1, A2, B1, B2, A3 and A4.

Eighth Row: Work strand C2 over strands A1, A2, B1, B2, A3, A4 and C1.

Now you have worked one complete color pattern (see Diagram 7). Continue repeating this eight row color pattern until your Friendship Bracelet is long enough to fit around your wrist.

Diagram 7

When your Bracelet has been made to desired length, tie all eight strands together in a knot as in Diagram 1. Trim tail to same length as beginning tail.

Now comes the best part of all — wearing your Friendship Bracelet! Tie it around your wrist using a square knot (right tail over left tail, then left tail over right tail) . . . and make a friend today!

Helpful Hints:

Try to keep the eight strands separated while working to prevent them from tangling near the bottom.

Maintain an even tension when tightening knots throughout Bracelet. A tighter tension will result in a stiffer bracelet while a very loose tension could cause holes between the double knots. Find the tension that looks most attractive to you.

You can make an endless variety of Friendship Bracelets with the 360 colors available in DMC Embroidery Floss. Wide stripes, narrow stripes, multi-colored, all one color — the choice is yours. DMC Embroidery Floss and your imagination — together they can create great Friendship Bracelets!

The DMC Corporation
107 Trumbull Street
Elizabeth, NJ 07206

Fig. 5.2. Friendship bracelet instructions.

- Refer to the colored plates on pages 17–23 of *Folk Stories of the Hmong* that show the traditional Hmong necklace. Have the students design an original necklace and illustrate it.

- Brainstorm for other materials that could be used to create jewelry.

- Instruct students to silently observe three people in the classroom and list all of the jewelry they are wearing.

CREATING TEXTILES

Examine the *pa ndau* pictures (figures 5.3–5.9). Figure 5.3 illustrates many activities: clearing a field; planting hemp seeds among the remaining tree stumps; harvesting, drying, and stripping the hemp; spinning it into thread and dying the yarn; weaving the fabric; cutting out pieces of fabric for clothing; sewing the clothes; taking crops to the family storage building; and grinding the grain to make flour.

Fig. 5.3. *Pa ndau* showing cutting the trees; planting hemp seeds; harvesting, drying, and stripping the hemp; winding fiber and spinning it into thread; dying and drying the yarn; weaving fabric; cutting fabric for clothing; sewing clothes; taking crops to the family storage building; and grinding grain into flour.

Fig. 5.4. Stripping the hemp plant to start the fiber-making process.

Fig. 5.5. Winding the fiber.

Fig. 5.6. Spinning the fiber into thread.

Fig. 5.7. Weaving the fabric on the loom.

Fig. 5.8. Cutting pieces from the fabric and sewing them into clothes.

Fig. 5.9. Hmong family taking the garden crops to their storage building.
51Wx99H

✔ DISCUSSION AND ACTIVITIES

♦ Have students illustrate what an American farmer does when he grows a cotton crop and harvests it. Discuss the steps they could include.

♦ Instruct students to illustrate the steps involved in planting an apple tree, collecting the apples, canning them, making cider, making applesauce, and baking pies.

♦ An example of a creative way to tell and illustrate how to make applesauce is the picture book *Rain Makes Applesauce* by Julian Scheer and Marvin Bileck.

TRADITIONAL HMONG MUSIC AND MUSICAL INSTRUMENTS

Music has been around forever. Early people believed that music was magic and could carry messages to the spirit world. Today, some people still believe that this is so. Each person who experiences music has his or her own idea as to what music is and what it does for all of us.

Music, singing, playing, and dancing are part of the traditions of every culture. We play music; dance, march, or move to music; sing with music; and tell stories with and about music. We even play games to music, such as musical chairs. From the bagpipers in India to military bands, music has even served to inspire participants in battle.

Stone Age hunters used a musical bow to hypnotize their prey. When an arrow was released from their bow, it created a humming sound. By adding strings of different lengths and widths to the bow, it became a musical harp.

Ancient Athenians studied music as a discipline of mathematics, and during the medieval period, the trumpet was the coveted symbol of wealth and power and was outlawed for use by anyone except royalty and the upper Church hierarchy. When the black plague was at its height, the hurdy-gurdy was forbidden, because the plague seemed to follow the arrival of traveling minstrels who played the instrument. Removing the hurdy-gurdy was seen as a way of preventing the spread of the plague.

The Hmongs' music is an integral part of their lives. Music and poetry are major activities during courtships, marriages, funerals, and games during the New Year's festival. As in all cultures, the Hmongs' musical instruments are made from materials that are readily available. Drums are common instruments everywhere, including among the Hmong. Flutes also seem to be found worldwide. The Hmong make their flutes from bamboo.

Keng

An instrument commonly used during Hmong funerals is the *keng* (see figures 5.10–5.12). Some people describe the *keng* (or *kleng* or *qeej*) as a free-reed multiple pipe musical instrument while other people call it a bamboo mouth organ. Among the Hmong of Laos and Thailand, only men and boys play this instrument. But among the Hmong of China, both genders play it. It is a solo instrument played during social events, the New Year's festival, and leisure time. During funeral rituals the drum accompanies it.

It is played horizontally and is about two to five feet in length, depending on the preference and skill of the player. The *keng* is the only traditional Hmong musical instrument that can be played while dancing.

Fig. 5.10. *Keng* player.

Fig. 5.11. *Keng* player depicted on a *pa ndau*.

Fig. 5.12. Mice playing the funeral *keng* and drum.

For Hmong youth who want to learn how to play the *keng*, they must not only learn how to operate it but also learn to memorize all of the song texts that have passed from one generation to the next for centuries, especially the funeral recitations.

The Hmong view death as a long journey to life in another dimension where their ancestors live and then eventually are reincarnated. Thus, a dead person would need food, money, appropriate clothes, shoes, an umbrella, and animals (a horse to ride, which is symbolized by the parallel wooden structure that a corpse is laid on, plus chickens, pigs, and cows that were sacrificed during the funeral).

During the funeral, the *keng* is used to communicate with or speak to the dead person and any other spirits. There are song texts that the *keng* player must follow in each step. For example, after a person dies, has been cleaned or washed and dressed in burial clothes, the *keng* player would begin the first ritual by playing a recitation called "Showing the Way." It is an instruction for the journey to the ancestors and an explanation of the creation of the world and why death must occur. After the "Showing the Way" is performed, the "Song of Expiring Life" follows. This song tells the dead person that he or she is really dead and that they need to go to find their ancestors. It gives instructions for the dead person to follow.

Today, only the Hmong who still maintain their traditional religion use the *keng* during a funeral. The Hmong who have become Christians or converted to other forms of worship have abandoned the use of the *keng* in their funerals. Instead, they would have a sermon where people pray together rather than a traditional funeral with the *keng* and funeral drum played loudly throughout the day.

Mouth Harp

The mouth harp has romantic connotations and is used for serenades and courting and is considered by some so irresistible that playing it is forbidden during harvest time when people's minds must not be distracted from their work. For some peoples, the mouth harp functions as a kind of love letter and proposal rolled into one. A youth plays the instrument at a girl's house and sometimes leaves the instrument there. If the girl accepts the gift of the mouth harp, she has symbolically accepted the marriage proposal of her suitor.

The mouth harp is played by both males and females and during courtship at night. When the boyfriend plays the courting music, the girlfriend may reply to him by playing a mouth harp from her bedroom or she can whisper to him about her feelings toward him. Because the mouth harp produces a soft and gentle music that is not much louder than a whisper, it is used mostly among courting people to chat in the evenings of their peak courtship time.

Mouth harps are made to produce a variety of different notes and sounds by changing the size and shape of the mouth. The mouth harp has a flexible blade. The person playing it moves his mouth to cause different overtones. These instruments can be whittled out of a single piece of bamboo but are commonly made from a forged iron frame fitted with a steel tongue.

Leaf Blowing

A common instrument used by both males and females is a blade of grass or plant leaf held between the thumbs. The Hmong "leaf blow" their music during their leisure time or when they travel on the road between their homes and their farms. Leaf blowing is done mostly during the day to express feelings.

Violin

The one-string violin (*xim xaus*) is played mostly by men and boys during leisure time, courtship, and the New Year's festival (see figures 5.13 and 5.14). Today, there are very few Hmong in the United States who know how to play this instrument. It usually can be seen played once a year at the New Year's party.

Flutes

There are three types of Hmong flutes. They are the reed flute (*daj nplaim*), leaf flute (*daj plooj*), and the bamboo flute with five or six finger holes (*daj pwm liv*). In Asia, both men and women played these flutes during their leisure and courtship time. In Laos, people would play these instruments as they were walking from their homes to their fields. They created the most wonderful music when these flutes were accompanied by the voices of singing tropical birds and insects. But in the United States, the Hmong only play these flutes at parties or inside their homes. If they sit on their porches and play them, neighbors have often criticized their music because they do not like it or understand the music.

Songs

Traditional folk songs are sung during the New Year's festival, leisure time, traveling between home and the fields, or whenever someone asks that they be sung. There are folk songs on many different topics. For example, there are songs about the process of becoming a daughter-in-law or about life as a daughter-in-law (*kwv txhiaj ua nyab*). These songs talk about how challenging, hard, and miserable some daughters-in-law's lives can be.

The love songs (*kwv txhiaj plees*) tell about all aspects of love, loving relationships, or broken hearts. They cover all topics of love-related experiences and feelings that people can express or create.

The orphan songs (*kwv txhiaj ntsuag*) are about children who have lost their parents during childhood and how hard it is for them without parents who love and care for them. These songs can also include a husband or wife who has lost a spouse. These kinds of songs talk about how much the person misses his or her partner or about how life has been without them around.

The death songs (*kwv txhiaj tuag*) tell about how people die, where they go, and what happens during their funeral. They include whether the deceased has a brother, sister, or parents around to make sure they receive all the necessities they need on their journey to the other life.

The migration songs (*kwv txhiaj tsiv teb tsaws chaw*) tell about how the Hmong or individual singers have moved from place to place, country to country, who and what they left behind, and how much they miss their old places and their families and friends.

Fig. 5.13. Musician playing the one-string violin.

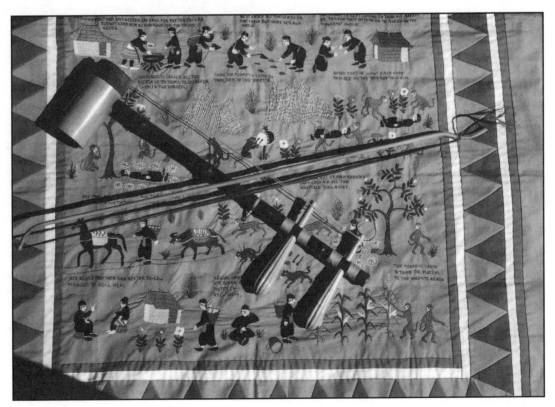

Fig. 5.14. One-string violin.

CONTEMPORARY HMONG MUSIC
AND MUSICAL INSTRUMENTS

All of the above discussions are about traditional Hmong music. Most of them still prevail in the Hmong communities in the United States but fewer Hmong are able to play the instruments or sing the songs. The older generations are forgetting the Hmong music because they do not have many chances to play or hear the songs. The younger Hmong generations are not interested or are too busy in school and work to have much time to learn the centuries-old traditional music that takes so much time, patience, and effort to master.

Today, the Hmong have incorporated all kinds of modern music to entertain themselves (figure 5.15). Hmong youth today play guitar, piano, drum, the Western violin, organ, and other types of modern musical instruments better than they can play a Hmong reed flute, *keng*, or mouth harp or practice leaf blowing. There is more contemporary Hmong music with modern instruments for sale at the Hmong grocery stores than traditional Hmong music. At the Hmong New Year's festival, the Hmong modern music is played louder and more frequently than the traditional Hmong music. When the Hmong youth today listen to American music or contemporary Hmong music, they dance, laugh, and enjoy themselves because they can relate to it and understand it. Yet when they listen to traditional Hmong music, they say it is boring and nonsense because they do not understand or appreciate it.

Fig. 5.15. Modern amplified musicians playing for a Hmong New Year's celebration.

✔ DISCUSSION AND ACTIVITIES

- Ask the students what they think about the changing ways and forms of music that the young Hmong appreciate.

- Brainstorm with the students about what kinds of musical instruments they can make from common materials.

- Share *ABC: Musical Instruments from the Metropolitan Museum of Art* by Florence Cassen Mayers (New York: Harry N. Abrams, 1982). Notice the range of complexity of the instruments.

- Visit a crafter of musical instruments. (Your local musical instrument store might be able to provide names of local instrument makers to visit.) Have students find out how this person got started making instruments, what his or her favorite instrument is and why.

- Take the students on a nature walk to find nature instruments. Have them use seed pods as shakers. Use sticks as percussive instruments. Blow on a leaf or blade of grass held between your thumbs. Make reeds into whistles. They can also grow gourds and let them dry several months. The seeds will rattle inside, making shakers.

- Take the students on a listening trip to observe the music of nature. Sit by a stream, listen to crickets and locusts, identify different bird songs, or write a poem about the sounds of the wind.

- Have the students collect a file of pictures of different flutes and pan pipes from around the world. Make a chart listing the name, country, type of instrument, size, material, number of holes, and other characteristics of each instrument.

- Have the students experiment with various materials for flute making, such as straws, reeds, pipes, bamboo, macaroni, and so forth. How does the placement of holes affect the musical scale?

- Have the students experiment with vibration, sound, and pitch using a variety of materials.

- Encourage experimenting with sounds. Have the students use clay pots, bottles of assorted sizes and shapes, nails and bolts, aluminum pipes and pot lids, bones, pieces of wood that are of different lengths, and other objects to hang as wind chimes. One musician in Colorado has used wrenches hung from a rod for a wrench chime.

- Have the students create their own drums from a variety of materials.

SYMBOLISM IN HMONG FOLK ART

In the arts of the Hmong we find many examples of the use of symbols. Symbols in most cultures can be traced to a time before a majority of people could read and write. Everything stood for something—if you had the "right dictionary," you could read the symbols. Colors were significant as well as the designs themselves.

The *pa ndau* designs contain traditional, highly symbolic patterns. For instance, the snail is a symbol of family growth and interrelatedness. The center of the coil of the snail's shell symbolizes the ancestors. The outer spirals are the successive generations, and the double snail shell represents the union of two families and also symbolizes the spinning motion used in many spiritual chants (see figure 5.16).

Shapes of designs, expressions of nature, and spiritual depictions all have specific meaning. One caution, though, is that diversity is one of the most salient characteristics of the Hmong. For instance, different groups may have different interpretations for designs that are considered the "real" ones. The overall pattern of the symbols, however, is common to all groups.

Fig. 5.16. Snail shell, which symbolizes family and growth.

Symbols of Creatures

Creatures are often depicted as symbols. The following list provides examples of this and are found on many stitchery works.

- ♦ Centipedes are known for medicinal qualities and are highly respected (see figure 5.17).

- ♦ Snails are a symbol of family growth and interrelatedness. As mentioned earlier, the center of the coil of the snail's shell symbolizes the ancestors. The outer spirals are the successive generations and the double snail shell represents the union of two families as well as the spinning motion used in many spiritual chants (see figures 5.16, 5.18, and 5.19).

- ♦ Tracks can be considered the spirit imprints of the person or animal who has passed by. For example, tiger paw prints can represent spirit imprints. Spirits of people were sometimes thought to have been taken over by tigers. The soul of the spirit tigers might turn into an evil spirit called a magic soul-tiger. A magic soul-tiger could be recognized because it had five toes instead of the four toes found on a real tiger.

Fig. 5.17. Centipede, which is valued for its medicinal qualities.

Fig. 5.18. Fireworks and snail shells.

Fig. 5.19. Snail shells and dog foot corners.

♦ Butterflies may be the souls of the dead.

♦ The rooster is a feisty protector. It also is the bird who awakens the sun at dawn.

♦ The toad lives on the moon and is connected to thunder.

♦ The crab covers the opening to the sky that permits the floodwaters to flow.

♦ The tortoise brings advice from the spirit world and ancestors to people on earth.

♦ The grasshoppers, according to one tale, were the first living things on earth. The sky spirit was dissatisfied because he thought the grasshoppers were stupid, so he created humans.

♦ The bear was feared.

♦ The woodpecker could pull worms and caterpillars from the growing bamboo spirit.

♦ If a bird flies into a house and roosts, it is a warning or a bad omen.

♦ If a snake enters the house, it is a sign that someone in the family will die soon.

♦ Elephants are respected for their strength and the Hmong avoid saying anything to hurt them lest elephants come and damage a family's property. Some say that elephants lead dead spirits to the otherworld and a particular black hoof on the elephant symbolizes whether the dead spirit is a mother, father, sister, or brother.

♦ Spiders were not removed from the home. Their webs were used medicinally. Figure 5.22 is a representation of a spider web.

♦ Dragons were thought to be snakes that grew huge and lived in and guarded the waters. The protective armor of the dragon represents the mythical dragon that lives forever, never knows sickness, and is respected by all.

✔ DISCUSSION AND ACTIVITIES

♦ As a class, examine the *pa ndau* examples in *Folk Stories of the Hmong*. Ask the students if they can identify any of the listed creatures.

♦ Have the students draw pictures using symbols to represent the members of their families.

♦ Have the students draw tracks of people or animals that might have walked in the school yard.

Fig. 5.20. Elephant's foot and plume design. The elephant's foot is the imprint of the most powerful good spirit. The plume design is associated with great wealth.

Fig. 5.21. Elephant's foot and dog's foot designs.

Fig. 5.22. Spider web with a variety of borders.

- Instruct your students to write a story about creatures that they love. They can illustrate their stories with symbols to represent these creatures.

- Students could write a story about creatures they fear and illustrate it with symbols representing them.

- Bring to class examples of emblems, shields, and other symbols of knights. Have students "read" these objects to gain information about the knight. Then have students create their own family crest, emblem, or shield. They could also create one as their own personal representation.

- As a class, examine the map and flag of Laos on page 25 in *Folk Stories of the Hmong*. Discuss what the symbols on the flag stand for. (The three elephants [white figures enclosed in red squares in the two upper corners] represent the three rulers of the land in the southern, central and northern regions.) Discuss the symbols used on the United States flag.

- Have students brainstorm about creatures they admire and represent them with symbols. Encourage the students to share with others and discover things they didn't know about their classmates.

Other Symbols

The Hmong also used geometric designs and representations from plants in their decorations. The following list gives some examples.

- Triangles are used to represent teeth, fish scales, dragon scales, fences, mountains, or protective barriers to keep good spirits in and evil spirits out.

- A diamond in a square can represent the altar maintained in the home, mountains, or the imprint of the most powerful good spirit (see figure 5.23). It also could be the floor plan of a Buddhist pagoda.

- The dream maze is a pattern of right-angles appliqués (see figure 5.24). Legend has it that a Hmong woman awoke from a dream to cut out this new and different pattern.

- The pumpkin seed and snail pattern is used on children's hats. It is thought that young souls tend to wander and that this pattern bonds a child's soul to its head until the soul is used to being in a new environment.

- A fish hook symbolizes a young girl's hope of finding a suitor.

- An eight-pointed star, which is sometimes referred to as the "left star," indicates good luck and is a protective symbol (see figure 5.25).

- An ancient, universal symbol, the swastika represents good fortune. It is formed by an equal-armed cross with the ends of the arms bent at right angles. (Today the swastika is often associated with Nazi Germany, which adopted the emblem in 1935.)

Fig. 5.23. Elephant's foot with diamonds in a square. Diamonds in a square can represent an altar or mountains.

Fig. 5.24. Dream maze with the happiness-for-all symbol.

Fig. 5.25. Star with snail shell and heart motif.

♦ Other symbols used are hearts, crosses, spinning wheels, and ram's heads (see figures 5.25–5.28).

♦ Stories tell of a symbol for "enough" when a woman feels she has given birth to as many children as she intends to have. By using the symbol on her clothing, she announces that idea.

Fig. 5.26. Heart design.

Fig. 5.27. Centipede border with crosses and spinning wheel design.

Fig. 5.28. Ram's head, elephant's foot, and heart motif.

✔ DISCUSSION AND ACTIVITIES

◆ Have students use shapes to make some designs that symbolize an idea.

◆ Hmong symbols are used in decorations. Have students create decorations using the symbols they designed.

◆ As a class, study advertisements. Have students collect examples of the use of symbols in advertising.

◆ Discuss how cartoons and cartoon characters use symbols. Have students make a collection of these samples.

◆ Look at a catalog that features jewelry and make a list of the symbols you find there.

◆ Symbols can be found by every culture in the world. Egypt is a good example. Find some books on Egypt and discover all of the buildings, monuments, and art carved with hieroglyphs. Have students make a list of the symbols they find.

◆ Native Americans have left complex communications, messages, maps, and other information on rocks, canyon walls, and their buildings. Collect pictures and information on pictographs and petroglyphs. Discuss the messages you find in them.

◆ Symbols or logos are used to identify cities, states, and countries. Have students make collections of what they can find.

◆ What other symbols from other cultures can students find? Have them share their discoveries with each other.

◆ Road signs use many symbols. If possible, get a copy of your state's driving manual and check through it for symbols.

COLORS

Language is filled with color metaphors. Here are just a few:

green with envy	red tape
a white heat	golden years
a white lie	black despair
purple passion	black sheep
purple prose	blue blood
a purple funk	silver lining
a red herring	someone who is yellow
a red letter day	everything is just rosy

Colors are symbols for emotion, circumstance, and experience. Most cultures are filled with examples of the use of black to symbolize evil and wickedness and white to symbolize goodness and purity. In many cultures, the colors of the rainbow are significant and magical. The Greeks believed that color was the manifestation of universal harmony. From early times people associated color with creation and the workings of divine forces.

There are cultural differences for the use of colors to represent the same feelings. Examples of this are mourning colors. In China, it is white; in Egypt it is yellow; in Thailand it is purple; in South Africa it is red; and in Iran, it is blue. The Hmong wear white headbands for death and mourning. The colors red and black are used in Hmong funeral clothes. The Sioux use green at funerals.

In Tibetan prayer flags used on mountains, homes and temples throughout Nepal and Bhutan, there are five different colored flags, each printed with prayers. The five colors are red, green, yellow, blue and white, which represent the five elements: earth, water, fire, air, and ether.

Names of colors most likely emerged as humans associated an identifying quality to a particular thing or object. References to color that depend upon knowledge of an object are quite common. These include: sky blue, snowy white, blood red, beet red, fire engine red, lime green, emerald green, coal black, pitch black, and lemon yellow.

Red is the color of direction. The Pharaoh's flat red crown represented the dominion of Lower Egypt and the east. Red, for the Hopi and the Chinese, stands for the south. The Hopi and Tibetan color symbol for the north is yellow. To the Tibetans, red represents the west. Red is also the color of the Red Corn Mother of the Pueblo, and her home is in the south. Green represents east in China and west for the Hopi. Purple signified the east for people of ancient Ireland. Blue represented south for the Tibetan and north for the Navaho.

Color appeared to the ancients to have supernatural, transformative properties. It was something of mystical significance, spiritual potency, magical force, and divine meaning. Color plays a primary role even today in rituals and rites and is a principal feature of the contents of common folklore and wisdom, language, and metaphor.

✔ DISCUSSION AND ACTIVITIES

♦ Have students investigate the significance of red eggs. Many cultures associate them with the regeneration of life and Easter traditions. How does this relate to American Easter eggs?

♦ Have students research why Norse runes are rendered in red.

♦ As a class, examine calendars. Are there days marked in red because they are considered sacred or special days?

♦ Many holidays, such as Christmas, Valentine's Day and the Fourth of July, are represented by red. Red is also associated with the Chinese New Year and signifies good luck. Discuss with the students how they think these events are related.

- Have students research the colors of dresses worn by brides throughout the world. Challenge them to find examples of white, red, and black wedding dresses.

- Have students discover and discuss why white robes are worn by religious leaders.

- Interview a museum curator to learn why the dead were encased in gold in Egypt and Asia.

- Interview members of various clergy to find out about the color purple and its association with Easter as well as its significance to royalty or imperial rule. In Jewish ceremony, purple represents splendor and dignity whereas in Catholic worship it represents suffering and endurance. Find out if the members of the clergy have any ideas as to why this is.

- In the movie *Braveheart*, why were the Scotsmen painted blue when they entered battles?

- Gemstones were believed to be curative agents, partly because of their colors. Have the students research gemstones. They should find out each gem's color and what curative properties it was believed to have. Recently, spirit beads or "power" beads used in bracelets have become popular. The beads represent moods and attributes such as success, love, contentment, energy, self control, courage, and strength.

- Examine the regional clothing of the Hmong. What are the prominent colors used?

6

Customs and Symbols

NEW YEAR'S FESTIVAL

The New Year's festival is the high point of village life and is anticipated all year. In each village, the heads of clans, who are always the eldest men, meet to arrange the event. Each village plans its festival to take place at a different time so that villagers can invite one another to their activities.

The New Year's festival is often the beginning of intense courtship in which young people select and woo their mates. Wearing their finest embroidered clothes and silver jewelry, young men and women pair off and toss soft cloth balls back and forth to each other. Anyone who drops the ball must forfeit a gift (to be returned later) or sing a folk song. Later, the young man might visit the girl's house. He might whisper to her through the woven bamboo wall and play music on a small mouth harp. These activities begin a process of courtship that culminates in a raft of marriages following the New Year's celebration.

Each person is expected to wear new clothes for the festival to show that the new year will be a good, rich one. This custom might be compared with the need for new clothes for an Easter celebration. Both holidays are timed for the new growing season.

MARRIAGE CUSTOMS

Following the New Year's festival celebrations, many couples get married. In Laos, when a Hmong boy and girl wished to marry, at least two elders from each of their extended families, or clans, would meet. They would either approve of the marriage or not. If it was approved, they would negotiate the bride price, usually paid in silver, and then make the arrangements for the wedding. The bride price was paid by the groom's family to hers to acknowledge the new value a wife brings to a man.

The parents of the bride then held a feast of roasted pig to celebrate the official announcement of marriage. During the wedding feast, if the young man had abducted his bride without having negotiated with her family, his mother-in-law would accost him with a stick an or oral insult. No matter how she scolded or hit him, he would continue to beg to show that he was serious and would be loyal to her daughter.

After the wedding ceremonies and banquet, the souls and good fortune of the young couple were symbolically wrapped up inside an umbrella that was tied with the band that had been wrapped around the turban of the bride. The umbrella was carried in a procession to the groom's house. A banquet there was followed by the *baci* ceremony, in which strings were tied around the wrists of the young couple with blessings and good wishes (see figures 6.1–6.2).

Fig. 6.1. Ball playing at the New Year's festival followed by a wedding group.

Fig. 6.2. Wedding ceremonies.

Normally, as the bride entered the groom's house for the first time, a rooster was waved over her to symbolize that she was now a member of the groom's household (see figure 6.3).

✔ DISCUSSION AND ACTIVITIES

♦ Make soft balls like the ones used in the New Year's festival ritual. Next, form two lines that face each other—one with boys and one with girls. The students should toss the ball back and forth to the people across from them.

Create a song to sing if the ball is dropped.

What gift would be forfeited if the ball was dropped?

Have each student write a poem to recite if he or she drops the ball.

♦ Invent other possible activities for a New Year's festival.

♦ Ask students to discuss what blessings and wishes they would make during the *baci* ceremony for a young couple.

Fig. 6.3. Shaman holding the rooster over the wedding couple to symbolize that the bride is now a member of the groom's household.

Fig. 6.4. This healing ceremony with the sacrifice of a pig is another important family ritual. The sick person is sitting while the shaman performs healing rituals at the family altar.

- Have students investigate wedding customs in a variety of cultures. How are they alike? How are they different?

- Discuss weddings that your students have attended. What customs did they observe?

- Research Native American cultures, and find out what some of their wedding traditions are. Compare and contrast them with Hmong customs.

- Examine the picture of the *pa ndau* that shows the sequence and details of a Hmong wedding. Ask your students: Does this picture explain the wedding better than words do?

- For an art activity, have the students draw their own sequence and details of a courtship and a wedding they might attend.

- Have the class research wedding lore and customs. For example:

  Why are there wedding attendants? In America, why does the bride wear a white gown? What is the history of the wedding ring? Why do people throw rice on the couple after the wedding? What does the wedding cake symbolize? Why does the groom carry the bride over the threshold on the wedding night? What is the historical purpose of the honeymoon?

  In African-American weddings, why does the bride wear a veil of braided hair over her face? Why is *kente* cloth worn? What is the jumping-the-broom ritual? What kinds of gifts are given to the couple or from the couple to the attendants?

  In Italy, why are candy-covered almonds presented to the wedding guests? What is the wedding bag used for by the bride?

  In Hispanic weddings, what is the symbolism of a lasso, a figure eight rope? Why does the groom present thirteen gold coins to his bride?

  Why do the Irish strew flower petals? What are the traditional foods served at an Irish wedding? What can you discover about the "jaunting chair" used at an Irish wedding reception.

  At a French wedding, why are laurel leaves spread outside the church when the wedding couple departs? What color is everything at a French wedding?

  At a Chinese wedding, why is lucky money presented in red envelopes? Why are red and gold used for Chinese wedding invitations, decorations, and gift wrapping? Why do the Chinese set off firecrackers in the couple's path?

  In a Jewish wedding, what is the *mikeva* and the *chuppah*? Why does the groom stomp on a glass at the end of the ceremony?

GAMES AND TOYS

Pretend you are a traditional Hmong child in Laos. Learn all you can about the climate and geography of Laos. What is the weather like? What grows there? What work do the people do? What animals do they use to help them do it? What natural materials are available to use in making utensils, musical instruments, building houses, and so on? (Study the *pa ndau* for ideas.)

Kao Xiong's Childhood Memories of Play

When I was a boy, I lived with my grandfather, grandmother, aunt, and uncle in a Hmong village called Hoi Xa Veng located in Xieng Khuang province in Laos. My father died when I was a baby. My mother remarried and moved away to live in another village. She died a few years later.

According to Hmong custom, I had to live with my father's family when he died. My grandparents, aunts, and uncles all helped raise me. When I was little, I slept with my grandparents. My grandfather would hold me close to him as we slept. He kept me warm and made sure the blanket covered me when it was cold at night.

I had a lot of aunts and uncles who would come and take me places with them. Many times I slept with them also. When they cooked a special dish or had a feast, they either invited me to eat with them or they would save some and bring the food for me to eat later. I was happy.

When I was about ten years old, I often went to the house of one of my aunts and played with her children for a few days. Sometimes, I would go without asking for my grandparents' permission. When I came back I would gather some big pieces of firewood and carry them home. When I arrived at home, I made sure they saw me carrying the firewood before I put it away. If they did not see me, I would continue to hold the firewood on my shoulder until they saw me. When they saw me with all the firewood, they were pleased and I felt relieved.

One of the games that I enjoyed playing was the spinning top (*ntaus tuj lub*). When I was a little boy, my grandfather made a little wooden spinning top for me. I would carry it with me all the time. I would feel it with my hands while I watched the older boys spinning tops. When I was about two to three years old, I would play the spinning tops with other boys my age. When I was little, I played with a small spinning top, and as I grew older I played with bigger ones. When I became an adult in Laos I still played spinning top games, but then I played with very big spinning tops.

During my teenage years I loved to play a Hmong game called "hitting the teepee" (*ntaus tshuav*). My teenage male relatives and I would go to cut firewood together. We usually made an agreement about the kind of firewood that we would collect. Everyone would collect the same kind. Each one of us gathered as much firewood as we could carry. When we got back to the village, we chose a flat area away from the houses and animals. We would decide the number of pieces of firewood each person would use to make a teepee-like structure. We would use three pieces of firewood to begin with and could go as high as we wanted. After we all agreed on a specific number, each of us used our own firewood and made a teepee-like structure. We made these teepees very close to each other.

After we all finished building our teepee-like structures, we stood next to one side of them. With two individual sticks that we had carved differently, we threw two sticks away from the buildings. Every person could throw his sticks as far or as close as he wanted. A person could also decide not to throw his stick and just say he wanted to wait, but each person could choose to wait only once. Each time, only one person could choose to wait, not two or three people.

The person whose sticks traveled the farthest distance was the one who had the first choice to throw his sticks back to hit the teepee structures. The person whose sticks landed closest to the teepees would wait to hit the structures last. As each person threw his sticks, he would position himself in the best way that he thought would help him to hit the buildings while his peers observed, laughed, and teased him. Each person took turns hitting the buildings with his sticks until all of them fell down. Each person would then get to keep the firewood that he hit when it fell to the ground.

Sometimes I would get a lot of firewood to carry home and I was thrilled. Then again, sometimes I got only a few pieces of firewood. If there were still some firewood pieces left, we would set up new structures and begin the game all over again. While we all played this game, we talked, laughed, teased each other, and had a really good time.

Based on this information and Hmong stories, have students invent some games and folk toys that they might play with if they lived in Laos. Instruct the students to look at the clues from the Hmong farming, hunting, and sewing activities. For instance, traditional Hmong hunters used bows and arrows to hunt (see figure 6.5). Small bows and arrows are made for the young boys to play with and practice with for hunting when they get bigger. Refer to the *pa ndau* picture of two boys chasing chickens (figure 6.6) and the one of the boy riding a water buffalo (figure 6.7). Are there similar pastimes that American children enjoy?

Fig. 6.5. Two Hmong boys with bows and arrows leaving for the hunt.

Fig. 6.6. Two children chasing chickens.

Fig. 6.7. Boy riding a water buffalo. One boy said, "In Laos when I was worried, riding the buffalo comforted me. In the United States I have no buffalo."

✔ DISCUSSION AND ACTIVITIES

♦ To make Hmong paper dolls and clothes to dress them in, first study the pictures of people wearing their traditional clothes in *Folk Stories of the Hmong*. Instruct students to draw and cut out figures of boys, girls, men, and women. Then, have the students illustrate the traditional clothes and make several drawings for outfits to fit the figures. The students can use these paper figures as props in telling Hmong stories.

♦ Have students make soft cloth doll figures. Clothe them with traditional Hmong outfits. Use exotic fabrics with lots of color and designs. They can also make jewelry for these soft dolls from aluminum, beads, and other objects you desire.

♦ Create a portable felt board by completely covering two hard boards that are eight by eleven inches. Sew a seam down the middle to act as a hinge. On the outside, wrap material around the boards to make pockets on each side for your felt story pieces. Attach handles to both ends of the boards for carrying. To secure it, add a five-inch tab from one pocket opening to the other pocket opening. The tab can be fastened with Velcro to the pockets.

Decorate the outside of one of the pockets with a felt decoration or figure. Also make felt people, plants, and other objects. These portable felt boards can be used for a variety of activities, such as telling stories or illustrating what you have learned.

♦ Have students make hats like the Hmong boys wear or decorate a girl's hat. Use these hats when you present plays, stories, or readers theatre productions.

♦ Make bean-stuffed dolls and objects for play.

♦ Create a folk game. Many folk games are made using bones and string or thongs. A pointed stick could be attached by string to a round bone with the object of the game being to catch the bone with the pointed stick.

♦ Make a toy using fruits, vegetables, and/or gourds.

♦ Balls can be used in games of throwing, kicking, or floating. Invent a new game using a ball.

♦ Make a kite with a Hmong design. Have a special kite-flying day where these kites are celebrated and enjoyed.

BUILDINGS AND HOMES

In the mountain regions, the homes and buildings are built on the ground with dirt floors and no windows (see figures 6.8 and 6.9). They have bamboo walls, tree poles, thatched roofs, and use no screws or nails. In the lowland areas, the Hmong build their buildings raised on poles. The reason for this is protection from flooding and unwanted creatures like snakes. Many times a floor of bamboo strips will be laid over the dirt for drainage.

Each home contains a stove and an open fire pit with family bedrooms along one wall. Traditionally, Hmong houses are built so that a distant mountain can be seen from either the front or the back door. The homes have lofts in a second story in which food is hung and stored. It is considered good luck to have a spider web in the house.

✔ DISCUSSION AND ACTIVITIES

♦ If possible, take your students to visit a house under construction. Discuss the process of building the house and what materials are used.

♦ Have students research how houses differ throughout the world. What would a house in Africa, Ireland, Finland, China, Japan, Mongolia, or Guatemala be made from?

♦ As a class, discover what kinds of homes the Plains Indians used.

♦ Ask: What are adobe houses and where are they common?

♦ Ask students to investigate if there are any good luck or religious symbols built into houses.

Fig. 6.8. Examples of Hmong buildings.

Fig. 6.9. Woman sitting in front of a house.

Bibliography

Adams, Nina S., and Alfred W. McCoy, eds. *Laos: War and Revolution.* New York: Harper and Row, 1970.

Anderson, Carolyn. *A Collection of Hmong Games.* Manitowoc, WI: C. J. Anderson, 1986.

Bernatzik, Hugo Adolf. *Akha and Miao: Problems of Applied Ethnography in Farther India.* Translated from German by Nagler Alois. New Haven, CT: Human Relations Areas Files Press, 1970.

Bettelheim, Bruno. *The Uses of Enchantment: The Meaning and Importance of Fairy Tales.* New York: Alfred A. Knopf, 1976.

Campbell, Margaret, Nakorn Pongoi, and Chusak Voraphitak. *From the Hands of the Hills.* Hong Kong: Media Transasia, Ltd., 1978.

Cha, Dia. *Dia's Story Cloth: The Hmong People's Journey of Freedom.* Stitched by Chue and Nhia Thao Cha. New York: Lee and Low, 1996.

Chan, Anthony, illus. *Hmong Textile Design.* Introduction by Norma J. Livo. Owings Mills, MD: Stemmer House, 1990.

Chase, Richard. *The Jack Tales.* Boston: Houghton Mifflin, 1943.

Chaturabhand, Preecha. *Peoples of the Hills.* Bangkok, Thailand: Editions Duang Kamol, 1980.

"A Clan Against All Odds," *Insight*, 16 January 1989.

Coburn, Jewell Reinhart. Illustrated by Tzexa Cherta Lee and Ann Sibley O'Brien. *Jouanah: A Hmong Cinderella*. Arcadia, CA: Shen's Books. 1996.

Cook, Sharon, and Jean Rusting. *Jouanah: A Hmong Cinderella Teacher's Guide*. Arcadia, CA: Shen's Books. 1996.

Dykstra, Anne H. *Flower Cloth of the Hmong*. Denver, CO: Denver Museum of Natural History, 1985.

Everyingham, J. "One Family's Odyssey to America." *National Geographic* 157, no. 5 (May 1980).

Fairservis, Walter A., Jr. *Costume of the East*. Denver, CO: Denver Museum of Natural History, 1971.

"Fighting Tribe." *Time*, 7 July 1961, 21–22.

Garrett, W. E. "No Place to Run: The Hmong of Laos." *National Geographic* 145, no. 1 (January 1974).

———. "Thailand, Refuge from Terror." *National Geographic* 157, no. 5 (May 1980).

Giacchino-Baker, Rosalie. *The Story of Mah: A Hmong "Romeo and Juliet" Folktale*. El Monte, CA: Pacific Asia Press, 1997.

Giacchino-Baker, Rosalie, Tina Bacon, and Kathy Felts. *Making Connections with Hmong Culture: A Teacher's Resource Book of Thematic Classroom Activities That Promote Intercultural Understanding*. El Monte, CA: Pacific Asia Press, 1997.

Goldfarb, Mace. *Fighters, Refugees, Immigrants: A Story of the Hmong*. Minneapolis, MN: Carolrhoda Books, 1982.

Hamilton-Merritt, Jane. *Hmong and Yao: Mountain Peoples of Southeast Asia*. Redding Ridge, CT: Survive, 1982. (For more information about this book, write to: Survive, P.O. Box 50, Redding Ridge, CT, 06876.)

———. *Tragic Mountains: The Hmong, the Americans, and the Secret Wars for Laos, 1942–1992*. Bloomington, IN: Indiana University Press, 1993.

Hassel, Carla J. *Creating Pa Ndau Appliqué*. Lombard, IL: Wallace-Homestead Book Company, 1984.

Hendricks, Glenn I., Bruce T. Downing, and Amos S. Deinard. *The Hmong in Transition*. Staten Island, NY: Center for Migration Studies of New York, Inc., 1986.

Herold, Joyce. *Flower Cloth of the Hmong*. Denver, CO: Denver Museum of Natural History, 1985.

Hmong Youth Cultural Awareness Project. *A Free People: Our Stories, Our Voices, Our Dreams.* Minneapolis, MN: Hmong Youth Cultural Awareness Project, 1994.

How-Man, Wong. "Peoples of China's Far Provinces." *National Geographic* 135, no. 3 (March 1984).

Johnson, Charles. *Myths, Legends, and Folk Tales from the Hmong of Laos.* St. Paul, MN: Macalester College, 1985.

Laufer, Berthold. "The Myth of P'an-Hu, the Bamboo King." *Journal of American Folklore*, vol. 30 (1917): 419–421.

Lemoine, J., and C. Mougne. "Why Has Death Stalked the Refugees?" *Natural History*, vol. 92 (November 1983): 6–19.

Lewis, Paul, and Elaine Lewis. *Peoples of the Golden Triangle.* London: Thames and Hudson, Ltd., 1984.

Livo, Norma J., and Dia Cha. *Folk Stories of the Hmong: Peoples of Laos, Thailand, and Vietnam.* Englewood, CO: Libraries Unlimited, 1991.

Livo, Norma J., and Sandra A. Rietz. *Storytelling Process and Practice.* Littleton, CO: Libraries Unlimited. 1986.

———. *Storytelling Activities.* Littleton, CO: Libraries Unlimited. 1987.

MacDowell, Marsha. *Hmong Folk Arts: A Guide for Teachers.* East Lansing, MI: Michigan State University, 1985.

McDowell, Bart. "Thailand: Luck of a Land in the Middle." *National Geographic* 162, no. 4 (October 1982).

Marshall, Elliot. "The Hmong: Dying of Culture Shock?" *Science*, vol. 212 (1981): 1008.

Mayers, Florence Cassen. *ABC: Musical Instruments from the Metropolitan Museum of Art.* New York: Harry N. Abrams, 1982.

Moore, David. *Dark Sky, Dark Land: Stories of the Hmong Boy Scouts of Troop 100.* Eden Prairie, MN: Tessera Publishers, 1989.

Moore-Howard, Patricia. *The Hmong: Yesterday and Today.* Sacramento, CA: Sacramento City Schools, 1987.

Morin, Stephen. "Troubled Refugees: Many Hmong Puzzled by Life in U.S. Yearn for Old Days in Laos." *Wall Street Journal,* 16 February 1983, 1, 25.

Mottin, Jean. *History of the Hmong.* Bangkok: Odeon Store, Ltd., 1980.

Murphy, Nora. *A Hmong Family.* Minneapolis, MN: Lerner Publications. 1997.

Olney, Douglas. *The Hmong and Their Neighbors.* CURA Reporter, University of Minnesota, Center for Urban and Regional Affairs. 8, no. 1 (1983): 8–14.

Peterson, Sally. "Translating Experience and the Reading of a Story Cloth." *Journal of American Folklore* 101, no. 399 (January/March 1988): 6–22.

Pulleyblank, E. G. "The Chinese and Their Neighbors in Prehistoric and Early Historic Times." *The Origins of Chinese Civilization.* Berkeley, CA: University of California Press, 1983.

Quincy, Keith. *Hmong: History of a People.* Cheney, WA: Eastern Washington University Press, 1988, 1995.

Ranard, Donald A. "The Last Bus." *Atlantic Monthly* (October 1987): 26–34.

Randall, Joan, ed. *Art of the Hmong-Americans.* Davis, CA: University of California Press, 1985.

Santoli, Al. *New Americans: An Oral History, Immigrants and Refugees in the U.S. Today.* New York: Viking, 1988.

Schafer, Edward H., et al. *Ancient China.* New York: Time-Life Books, 1967.

Scheer, Julian, and Marvin Bileck. *Rain Makes Applesauce.* New York: Holiday House, 1964.

Shea, Pegi Deitz. *The Whispering Cloth.* Illustrated by Anita Riggion and stitched by You Yang. Honesdale, PA: Boyds Mills Press. 1995.

Sherman, Spencer. "The Hmong in America." *National Geographic* 174, no. 4 (October 1988).

Snow, L. "Folk Medical Beliefs and Their Implications for Care of Patients." *Annals of Internal Medicine,* vol. 81 (1974): 82–96.

Sochurek, Howard. "Viet Nam's Montagnards." *National Geographic* 133, no. 4 (April 1968).

Social Security Administration, Office of Refugee Resettlement. "The Hmong Resettlement Study." Prepared by Literacy and Language Program, Northwest Regional Educational Laboratory, Portland, OR, 1984.

Trueba, Henry, Lila Jacobs, and Elizabeth Kirton. *Cultural Conflict and Adaptation: The Case of Hmong Children in American Society.* Bristol, PA: Falmer Press, 1990.

Vreeland, Susan. "Future of Laotian Folk Art Hangs by a Thread." *Christian Science Monitor* (November 19, 1981): 15.

———. "Through the Looking Glass with the Hmong of Laos." *Christian Science Monitor* (March 30, 1981): B13.

White, Peter. "Laos." *National Geographic* 171, no. 6 (June 1987).

———. "Mosaic of Cultures." *National Geographic* 139, no. 3 (March 1971).

White, Virginia. *Pa Ndau: The Needlework of the Hmong.* Washington, DC: Cheney Free Press, 1982.

Willcox, Donald. *Hmong Folklife.* Penland, NC: Hmong Natural Association of North Carolina, 1986. (For information about this book, write to : Don Willcox, P.O. Box 1, Penland, NC 28765.)

Xiong, Blia. *Nine-in-One, Grr! Grr!* Adapted by Cathy Spagnoli and illustrated by Nancy Hom. San Francisco, CA: Children's Press, 1989.

Xiong, Ia. *The Gift: The Hmong New Year.* El Monte, CA: Pacific Asia Press, 1996.

Audio Productions

Livo, Norma J., and Dia Cha. *Folk Stories of the Hmong: Peoples of Laos, Thailand, and Vietnam.* Englewood, CO: Libraries Unlimited, 1998, 60 minutes.

Video Productions

Livo, Norma J. *Hmong at Peace and War.* Sponsored by the Colorado Endowment for the Arts and Humanities and the University of Colorado at Denver, 1989, 15 minutes.

———. *Hmong Folklore.* Sponsored by Colorado Endowment for the Arts and Humanities and the University of Colorado at Denver, 1989, 15 minutes (also available in slide/tape format).

The Lost Country of Laos. Produced by Henry Castiel Productions.

Secrets of the Hmong. Produced by Henry Castiel Productions.

Threads of Survival. Produced by Vander Films, 21021 Green Hill Road #256, Farmington Hills, MI 48335.

Index

Activities. *See* Discussion and activities
Art techniques, 59–60

Baci. See String-tying ceremony
Bettelheim, Bruno, 28
Blessing, string-tying ceremony, 63
Bracelet, friendship, 64, 65
Buildings and homes, 98–99
   discussion and activities, 98–99

Cambodian Communist party, 27
Cha, Dia
   *Dia's Story Cloth: The Hmong People's
      Journey of Freedom*, 14
   memories, 8–14
Cinderella story, 36–39
   discussion and activities, 39
   "High-Tech Cinderella," 36–37
   variants, bibliography of, 38–39
Colors, 85–87
   discussion and activities, 86–87
Culture, 14–15
Customs, 89–93
   marriage customs, 90–93
   New Year's festival, 89

*Dia's Story Cloth: The Hmong People's Journey of
   Freedom*, 14
Dickens, Charles, 28
Discussion and activities
   buildings and homes, 98–99
   Cinderella stories, 39
   customs
      marriage, 91, 93
      New Year's festival, 91
   farming, 19–20
   folk arts
      color 86–87
      friendship bracelet, 64, 65
      jewelry, 64, 66
      music and musical instruments, 77
      pa ndau, 62
      string-tying ceremony, 64
      symbolism in, 80, 82, 85
      textile creation, 70
   food, 25–26
   games and toys, 97–98
   ghost stories, 53
   origins and history, Hmong people
      history, 6–7
      memories, Dia's, 14
      proverbs, 2
      riddles, 3

Discussion and activities (*continued*)
    stories and storytelling, 34–36, 49–50, 53
        Cinderella stories, 39
        illustrating activity, *Folk Stories of the*
            Hmong, 57–60
        writing stories, 55, 57

Enchanted Wood and Other Tales from Finland, The,
    39
Escape from Laos, Dia's memories of, 8–9

Fairy tales, 28–29
Farming, 17–20. *See also* Food
    discussion and activities, 19–20
Finger printing (art technique), 59
Flutes, 74
Folk arts, 61–87
    colors, 85–87
    jewelry, 64, 66
    music and musical instruments
        contemporary, 76–77
        traditional, 70–75
    pa ndau, 61–62
    string-tying ceremony, 62–64
    symbolism in, 78–85
    textile creation, 65–70
Folk songs, 74
Folk stories, 28–29
Folk Stories of the Hmong, 27
    illustration of story from, 57–60
    "Ngao Nao and Shee Na," 36
    "Orphan Boy and His Wife, The," 31–34
    pa ndau, sample, 62
    "Zeej Choj Kim, the Lazy Man," 45–49
Food, 20–26. *See also* Farming
    discussion and activities, 25–26, 57
    recipes, 24–25
Friendship bracelet, 64, 65

Games and toys, 94–98
    discussion and activities, 97–98
Geej. See *Keng*
Ghost stories, 50–53
Gutman, Dan, 36–37

"High-Tech Cinderella," 36–37
Histoire des Miao, 1

History of Hmong people. *See* Origins and
    history of Hmong people
Homes. *See* Buildings and homes

Illustrating stories, 57–60. *See also* Writing
    stories
    art techniques, 59–60
Immigrants, issues for Hmong people as, 14–15
Inspiration, 31

Jewelry, 64–66
    discussion and activities, 64, 66

"Kao Xiong's Childhood: Memories of Play,"
    94–95
Keng, 70–73
Khymer Rouge, 27
Kleng. See *Keng*

Language, 1–3
    lack of written, 1, 17, 31
Laos
    memories of, Dia's, 8–12
    storytelling in, 29
Leaf blowing, 74
Livo, George, 39
Livo, Norma, 39
"Love Ghost Story," 50–53
Ly, Fu, 28
Ly, Myhnia, 28

Marriage customs, 90–93
    discussion and activities, 91, 93
Meat dish (recipe), 24
Memories, Dia's, 8–14
    discussion and activities, 14
Miscellaneous Record of Yu
    Yang, The, 36
Mouth harp, 73
Music and musical instruments, 27
    contemporary, 76–77
    discussion and activities, 77
    traditional, 70–75

Neou, Kassie S., 27
New Mother's Menu (recipe), 25

New Year's festival, 89
"Ngao Nao and Shee Na," 36

Origins and history of Hmong people, 1–16
   history, 4–7
   immigrants, issues for Hmong people as, 14–15
   language, 1–3
   memories, Dia's, 8–14
   origins, 1–3
"Orphan Boy and His Wife, The," 31–34

Pa ndau, 61–62
   discussion and activities, 62
   illustration of "Ngao Nao and Shee Na," 36
Paper cutting (art technique), 59
Paper weaving (art technique), 59
Physical appearance, 3
Picture book creation, 60
Polystyrene printing (art technique), 60
Proverbs, 2

Qeej. See *Keng*

"Raising Rice," 17, 18
Recipes, 24–25
Refugee camp life, Dia's memories of, 13–14
Riddles, 2–3
   discussion and activities, 3
Rubbings (art technique), 59

Savina, F. M., 1, 3
Shaman, 15, 30
Singer, Isaac Bashevis, 30
Songs, 74–75
Soup (recipe), 24–25
Stenciling (art technique), 59
Stories and storytelling, 27–53
   Cinderella story, 36–39
      bibliography of variants, 38–39
      discussion and activities, 39

discussion and activities, 34–36, 49–50, 53
   elements of good, 55, 56
   stories, 27–29
      "High-Tech Cinderella," 36–38
      "Kao Xiong's Childhood: Memories of Play," 94–95
      "Love Ghost Story," 50–53
      "The Orphan Boy and His Wife," 31–34
      "Raising Rice," 17, 18
      "The Taiga Sampo, or The Magic Mill," 39, 40–44
      "Zeej Choj Kim, the Lazy Man," 39, 45–49
   storytelling, 29–34
   uses for, 27–28
   as wish fulfillment, 39
String block printing (art technique), 60
String-tying ceremony, 62–64
   discussion and activities, 64
Symbolism, 78–85
   creatures, 78–80, 81
      discussion and activities, 80, 82
   geometric designs and plants, 82–84
      discussion and activities, 85

"Taiga Sampo, or The Magic Mill, The," 39, 40–44
Textile creation, 65–70
   discussion and activities, 70
Thailand, Dia's memories of, 13–14
Tissue paper (art technique), 59
Toys. *See* Games and toys
Tracing paper (art technique), 59

Village life, Dia's memories of, 9–12
Violin, 74

Wood block printing (art technique), 60
Writing stories, 55–57. *See also* Illustrating stories
   discussion and activities, 55, 57–60
Written language, 31

"Zeej Choj Kim, the Lazy Man," 39, 45–49

from LIBRARIES UNLIMITED
and Its Division TEACHER IDEAS PRESS

FOLK STORIES OF THE HMONG
Peoples of Laos, Thailand, and Vietnam
Norma J. Livo and Dia Cha

The natural companion to *Teaching with Folk Stories of the Hmong*, this
bestselling title of the *World Folklore Series* offers 27 captivating tales
divided into three sections: beginnings; how-and-why stories; and tales of
love, magic, and fun. An audiotape is also available. **All Levels.**
xii, 135p. 7x10 cloth ISBN 0-87287-854-6

FOLKTALE THEMES AND ACTIVITIES FOR CHILDREN
Volume 1: Pourquoi Tales
Volume 2: Trickster and Transformation Tales
Anne Marie Kraus

Use the magical appeal of traditional how-and-why stories and fairy tales to
attract your students to a variety of related learning experiences. Used in a
planned sequence of story times, lessons, and activities, these stories lead
into motivational reading, prediction activities, Venn diagramming
comparisons, art projects, shadow puppetry, and more. **Grades 1–6**.
Vol. 1: xv, 152p. 8½x11 paper ISBN 1-56308-521-6
Vol. 2: xviii, 225p. 8½x11 paper ISBN 1-56308-608-5

MULTICULTURAL FOLKTALES
Readers Theatre for Elementary Students
Suzanne I. Barchers

Make traditional folk and fairy tales come alive. Representing more than 30
countries and regions, these 40 reproducible scripts (organized by grade
level) are accompanied by presentation suggestions and recommendations
for props and delivery. **Grades 1–5**.
xxi, 188p. 8½x11 paper ISBN 1-56308-760-X

GIFTED BOOKS, GIFTED READERS
Literature Activities to Excite Young Minds
Nancy J. Polette

What better way to stimulate gifted learners than with literature written by
gifted authors? Hundreds of beloved books are used as a basis for word
play, problem solving, creative writing, and more! **Grades K–8**.
xi, 282p. 8½x11 paper ISBN 1-56308-822-3

CELEBRATING THE EARTH
Stories, Experiences, and Activities
Norma J. Livo

Livo shows you how to use folk stories, personal narrative, and a variety of
learning projects to teach students how to observe, explore, and appreciate
the natural world. **All Levels**.
xvii, 174p. 8½x11 paper ISBN 1-56308-776-6

LIBRARIES UNLIMITED/TEACHER IDEAS PRESS
Dept. B017 • P.O. Box 6633 • Englewood, CO 80155-6633
Phone: 800-237-6124, ext. 1 • Fax: 303-220-8843
Web site: www.lu.com • E-mail: lu-books@lu.com